*The*Three Mathewsons

Christy and the Taming of Baseball's Early Ruffians

ROBERT D. GAINES

Hidden Shelf Publishing House
www.3mathewsons.com

Copyright © 2012. Robert Gaines
Hidden Shelf Publishing House
All rights reserved.

Library of Congress Cataloging-in-Publication Data

Gaines, Robert
The Three Mathewsons:
The Life and Family of Baseball's First All-America Idol

Includes bibliographical reference and index.

ISBN: 1475041098
ISBN-13: 978-1475041095

All photos courtesy of The Baseball Hall of Fame (Cooperstown, NY),
Bucknell University, and Keystone College.

Printed in the United States of America

Christy Mathewson was the greatest pitcher in baseball history, the first All-American hero, credited with forever changing the face of a tainted and brutal sport . . . loved for his athletic prowess, idolized for his unique character.

And his family was just as amazing . . .

CHAPTER ONE

Late November 1900 . . . Lewisburg, Pennsylvania

With a bag of old footballs at his feet, Christy Mathewson was standing alone in the middle of Loomis Field, seemingly lost in a deep gray dusk, shivering as the temperature once again tore below freezing.

Earlier, the wet and wind had traveled up the Susquehanna River from the south, a once tolerable rain having turned the field into a muddy mess, great for plowing through tackles, but lousy for dropkicking. Fortunately, he was able to find a few spots on the field that were still rock hard, lest the ball just sink into the muck.

Eyes down with deafening focus, Christy dropped the heavy football on its nose as his right foot made a clean and powerful strike, his strong leg adding lift and distance as the ball sailed high toward the west goal post, a good 40 yards to perfection . . . no problem.

As the last of six footballs plopped near the bottom of Bucknell Grove, Christy looked up the steep hill toward Old Main. He noticed that the mass of trees sprinkling the campus were now strangely barren, the once brilliant colors of the northeast autumn banished to the ground. In his third year at Bucknell, he still marveled at the beauty of the place and the academic majesty that he dearly loved.

Gathering the balls beyond the goal post, Christy decided to change course, brave the headwinds, and kick toward the east end of the field with a direct line toward Tustin Gym and the river. The new chemistry building was at his back as he punted each ball toward midfield, daring the winds to slow them down.

1

When the weather turned nasty, Coach George "Doc" Hoskins would often encourage Christy to go back to his dorm room at Old Main, get warm, and relinquish his kicking routine for just one day. In his mid-30s, the muscular and personable Hoskins loved playing the role of the "old coach." So, really, he should have known that "Rubber Leg" Mathewson would not leave the field until he had nailed at least 25 kicks from every conceivable distance and angle.

"Football weather, boys," Hoskins had grumbled to the team half an hour earlier. "They say it's good for the soul and makes you nasty. Well, let me just add that my hands and feet are freezing. Two more snaps and we're outta here."

"C'mon coach, I thought you were tough," laughed halfback Frank Stanton.

"Yeah, what could be better than an ice cold mud bath?" added Christy. "Life is good."

"No sun, no warmth," growled Hoskins, "I can't wait for basketball to start."

Stanton and Mathewson both grinned, a rare exchange between two teammates who at times allowed competitive jealousies to blur friendship. Still, they'd be obvious leaders for what should be a great Bucknell basketball team.

"Coach, let's just win at Villanova," said Christy, "and then we can think about the next sport."

"Glad to hear you say that, Mathewson," said the coach. "I was afraid you might already be dreaming about baseball."

"No Coach, my arm's too numb for baseball. I don't think I'll ever throw again."

"Yet another reason to go inside," said Hoskins as he turned to instruct the rest of the players, whose muddy spirits now seemed to have sunk deeper than their ankles. "Men, let's call it a day."

Hoskins turned back to his star player.

"And Mathewson, you go put that pitching arm under a blanket, and warm up your leg as well. We're going to need it in Philly."

"I will Coach, right after I take some extra field goals."

"Twenty-five?" asked Hoskins.

"At least," said Christy.

The team was already halfway to Tustin Gym as Hoskins turned away from Christy, the Bison coach shaking his head and smiling.

1900 Bucknell Bison with Christy (middle row, left) standing next to Frank Stanton.

The Bucknell eleven concluded the 1900 season with a scoreless tie at Villanova, never getting close enough to the goalpost for Matty to work his magic. The week before, however, he had kicked two field goals against Army at West Point, one a 48-yarder from a wicked angle. The powerful Black Knights had won the game 18-10, but sportswriter Walter Camp immediately alerted the nation of the prize Bison.

"Christy Mathewson is the finest drop kicker in intercollegiate competition," Camp wrote, adding that the 20-year-old junior was the nation's top punter, as well.

The legendary Camp, known as "the father of American football" was a great player in his younger days before coaching at Yale and Stanford.

When he retired in 1895, Camp had a phenomenal 79-5-3 coaching record, including three national championships at Yale. Now a sportswriter, Camp personally selected the All-America team at the end of each season.

Christy's biggest fan, however, was easily Jane Stoughton, a beautiful young woman who attended the Bucknell Female Institute.

"I can still see this tall, athletic body plowing through the Penn State line," Jane would say many years later. "Football was rough in those days and every time I would see Christy down, my heart would be in my mouth. But he would come up again, always charging forward."

In an era when touchdowns and field goals were each worth five points, Mathewson was a dangerous weapon. At 6-foot-2 and 180 pounds, he was lean, muscular, fast, and powerful. If he didn't run it into the end zone from his position as fullback, he could kick it through the posts. Even more, his long punts continually kept the opposition deep in its own territory.

But despite his prowess, the team had been rather disappointing. Sure, they had done well at home, whipping Wyoming Seminary, Williamsport, and Susquehanna by an aggregate score of 90-0. They also had topped Penn State for the second straight season. In '99, Matty's field goal had been the only score in a 5-0 Bucknell victory. This year, back on the first Saturday of November, the Orange and Blue had beaten the Nittany Lions 12-5.

Still, other than the deadlock at Villanova, the road had not been kind in '00, the Bison falling at Cornell, Duquesne, Lehigh, and Army.

The joke around campus was that if "Rubber Leg" was missing, he was likely out walking his *pet* football. In truth, Christy was seldom without the ball . . . even carried it to class. Plus, he could perform football tricks with undaunted grace. One involved rolling a football up his arm until his muscle methodically popped it back to his hand. It was a game he had practiced to precision using either arm.

Classmates were amazed, but not surprised. Christy was obsessed with perfection. Schoolwork, playing cards, kicking a football . . . he ruled the world of checkers and chess . . . thriving on competition, hard work, and pressure . . . never bending from the virtuous and healthy lifestyle he had followed since childhood.

Matty also was a young man of great promise and nagging immaturity. Wonderfully handsome, the "Big Man on Campus" was confident, driven, and brilliant in athletics and academics. Not so much in social circles, a kid stymied by an overwhelming shyness which classmates often confused for arrogance. Of course, it didn't help that Christy believed he was better than all of them.

But, really, how many Bucknellians had played major league baseball? Although, in the late fall of 1900, baseball was a prickly subject for Christy. It was bad enough that he had been called up in July to the pitiful last-place New York Giants and seldom given a chance to show his talent. The worst part was that most of his teammates seemed to hate him, to mock him, to purposely commit errors when he was on the mound . . . charging that he was nothing more than a bigheaded college boy.

Not to ease the situation, Christy didn't even bother to mask his belief that, yes, he was miles above this underachieving lot of illiterates.

At Bucknell, Christy shared a dorm room – 318 East Wing in Old Main – with fraternity brother Ernest Sterling, a gifted long distance runner flirting with a five-minute mile. Sterling also understood his roommate's true personality, the one that sometimes seemed hidden to other classmates. You see, Christy wasn't shy or aloof around his friends . . . he was pleasant, witty, interesting, and a lot of fun.

As if his mind wasn't always busy anyway, Christy had plenty to process over the school year. There was the baseball situation. And how could it possibly be that he was having trouble with one stupid course? He may have considered himself one of the premiere rock twirlers in the world, but he hated geology, recording a dismal 75 when the rest of his grades had never fallen below 90.

More important, certainly to Christy, was that he profoundly loved Jane Stoughton . . . with all his heart . . . the thought of her knocked him into a crazy giddiness. Jenny was beautiful, kind, fun, and a wonderful dancer. She also was a Sunday School teacher, which would definitely please Christy's mother.

Minerva Mathewson was still praying that her oldest son would some-day become a preacher. That hardly fit his current plan. Should baseball falter, Christy was considering a career in forestry, provided his future employers overlooked his keen dislike for geology.

Like any kid with big dreams, Christy Mathewson had no idea what was down the road. For starters, he did not know in late 1900 that he would soon become the greatest pitcher in baseball history. Forget the early bumps, Matty was but a couple of years from being idolized by mil-lions, the All-American hero and ultimate role model whose every move enhanced a legend from which he would never stumble. Along the way, he would be credited for almost single-handedly changing the national stereotype that professional baseball was a barbaric and tarnished game.

"He brought something to baseball that no one else had ever given the game," wrote famed sportswriter Grantland Rice. "He handed the game a certain touch of class, an indefinable lift in culture, brains, and personality. He is the only man I ever met who in spirit and inspiration was greater than his game."

First, a few statistics . . .

In a 17-year career, Christy would notch 373 victories against 188 defeats. Thirteen times he would top the 20-win mark, including four years with more than 30 victories. He completed 435 of the 551 games that he started while registering a phenomenal 2.13 earned run average. He notched 80 shutouts in his career and struck out 2,502 batters while issuing just over one base on balls per game.

Damon Runyon penned the oft-repeated observance: "Christy Mathewson pitched against Cincinnati yesterday. Another way of putting it is that Cincinnati lost a game of baseball. The first statement means the same as the second."

By 1903, Matty owned New York, the big city's first athletic superstar. Two years later, he rocked the entire nation. In the 1905 World Series, after his third straight 30-win season, Mathewson would demolish the powerful Philadelphia Athletics, champions of the American League, by throwing three shutouts in six days. It still remains the greatest pitching feat in World Series history. Although '05 would be their only world championship during Christy's reign, he would lead the Giants to five National League pennants and would retire with an abundance of records that would last for decades.

"He was the greatest pitcher who ever lived," said Connie Mack, who managed the Philadelphia Athletics for 50 years. "Matty had knowledge, judgment, perfect control, and form. It was wonderful to watch him pitch when he wasn't pitching against you."

In 1936, Matty would be one of the five charter members of the Baseball Hall of Fame, joining Ty Cobb, Babe Ruth, Honus Wagner, and Walter Johnson. One hundred years after he pitched, Christy Mathewson would be selected by Major League Baseball to its All-Century Team and *Sports Illustrated* followed in 2010 by naming him the greatest right-handed hurler in history.

But Matty's story would become far greater than an impressive ledger jammed with records and honors. Pure and simple, his was an uncharted journey of virtue and character that would forever change the game and the nation.

"He was an inspiration to everybody," said Baseball Commissioner Kenesaw Mountain Landis. "His sense of justice, his integrity, and sportsmanship made him far greater than Christy Mathewson the pitcher."

"He was the first truly national baseball figure who captured the country's admiration and hero worship by combining all the elements of baseball, religion, and American culture," wrote sports historian Donald Honig.

"We all knew that brain and brawn were combined here to an unusual degree," said Grantland Rice, "and beyond this a lofty idealism both on and off the field."

Yes, young Christy Mathewson would knock the world right between its polar caps. But that would be the future.

In the final days of 1900, Christy would have been content to simply map a path to one of America's newly established forest reserves. He could live on a mountaintop, marry Jenny Stoughton and raise a family, perhaps even someday write a novel . . . never throw another baseball.

CHAPTER TWO

Late summer 1883 . . . Factoryville, Pennsylvania

Outside the barn at their grandfather's farm, three-year-old Christy Mathewson was demonstrating to his young Aunt Jessie, age four, the fine art of twirling.

Christy had already been "seriously" pitching for more than a year, well schooled in the finer points of rock throwing . . . a master of control.

"The idea," he told Jessie, "is to hit the same spot with every pebble."

"I don't think we're supposed to be throwing rocks," said Jessie.

Christy seemed stunned at her concern. After all, his mother had told him that he should throw rocks away from the house . . . and never again throw dishes out the kitchen window . . . that's what she said and that was what he was doing . . . far from the kitchen . . . Jessica was such a baby.

"You gotta keep your eye on the target, Jessie," Christy instructed. "Wind up, keep your head still . . . and fire."

A perfect strike . . .

Unfortunately, today's target was the silky rear end of Grandfather's favorite horse, Dandy . . . and the old carriage horse was not happy.

Hearing Dandy's annoyance, Grandpa hurried from the house to the stable, the screen door slamming behind him. Storming past the two children and their pile of pebbles, Grandpa angrily grabbed a horse-whip that was hanging near the barn door. Dropping her rocks, Jessie bolted for the house. Young Christy, however, defiantly folded his arms and looked directly into the old man's fiery eyes.

"Wait a minute Grandpa," said the three-year-old, "let's talk this over."

Well, they did discuss the situation. Grandpa melted and Christy once again escaped a whipping . . . no comment from Dandy.

Young Christy in Factoryville.

Christopher Mathewson was born in northeast Pennsylvania on August 12, 1880. His would be a wonderful childhood, his parents – Gilbert and Minerva – providing a strong foundation with unwavering love.

When Christy was born, Joe Juneau was looking for gold in Alaska, Robert Louis Stevenson was writing *Treasure Island*, the British were at war in Afghanistan, and Billy the Kid was wanted dead or alive. But distant places were far beyond the reach of Factoryville, a small and quaint country village quietly resting in a beautiful and slender valley with plenty of fishing streams, apple orchards, cornfields, and shade trees. Located on the Delaware, Lackawanna & Western Railroad line; the borough of Factoryville numbered just under 700 residents with three churches and, ironically, no factories. It also had none of the coal dust that kicked up on the other side of the hills. The big city of Scranton was 15 miles to the southeast, a major journey in the late 19th century.

Tall and strong, Gilbert Mathewson was 33 years old when his first son was born. With an ancestry that backtracked from Rhode Island to England, Gilbert was a veteran of the Civil War, having enlisted as a 15-year-old private in the Second Regiment of Pennsylvania Heavy Artillery and fighting in Virginia at the Siege of Petersburg. After serving the Union cause for nearly two years, he returned to Factoryville, earning a living at various times as a postal worker, bar keeper, and land developer.

In 1878, Gilbert married Minerva Capwell, a lovely young woman eight years his junior. That was hardly an age gap; Minerva's parents had been separated in age by nearly four decades. George Capwell was 73 at his daughter's birth and dead by the time she entered elementary school.

A woman of strength and character, Minerva earned the nickname "Nervy" as a kid in reference to her prowess for breaking horses. She was 25 years old when Christy was born, bent on raising her family with an abundance of love, religion, and education.

Many years down the road, Minerva would recall, "I was always particular about regular hours of sleep and plenty of plain, wholesome food, good milk, fresh air, and the Golden Rule."

Of modest wealth, the Mathewsons lived in a pleasant and sturdy two-story home on a hill above town.

The oldest of four boys and two girls, Christy almost immediately demanded equal playing time with the older kids in town. At eight years old, he announced that someday he wanted to twirl baseballs for a living, which could only bring laughter. Folks had certainly heard of professional baseball and its highest level, the National League, but that was played in cities like New York, Chicago, and Philadelphia . . . a world away from Factoryville, where amateur town ball was the real game.

Still, to Christy's mind, the pro game of 1888 was wondrous. After all, these were the best ballplayers in the country. They played in huge stadiums on fields without rocks. Christy filed and remembered the slightest bit of news, memorizing the essential statistics of his favorite players – Cap Anson, Matches Kilroy, Silver King, Ice Box Chamberlain, Oyster

Burns, Pud Galvin, Sliding Billy Hamilton and Phenomenal Smith. Possibly because Christy had never actually seen any of them play, their greatness seemed unbounded.

The New York Giants, Chicago White Stockings, and Philadelphia Quakers were the best teams in the National League, although the Quakers were sometimes called the Phillies, which seemed a bit confusing. To Matty, each club was magical – the Pittsburgh Alleghenies, Boston Beaneaters, Detroit Wolverines, Indianapolis Hoosiers, and Washington Nationals. He also had heard about the American Association with the St. Louis Browns, Philadelphia Athletics, Brooklyn Bridegrooms, Cincinnati Red Stockings, Baltimore Orioles, and Cleveland Blues. He knew the Louisville Colonels were bad and that the way-out-west Kansas City Cowboys were worse.

Summertime brought a mixture of chores, church, swimming, fishing, reading, checkers, and One Old Cat (getting safely to base before the fielder nails you with the ball). But absolutely nothing topped playing real baseball with the older kids.

Not to brag, but Christy considered himself the greatest rock thrower in northeast Pennsylvania. Through continual practice, he had developed spot-on control . . . not that he didn't have to cough up a dollar for accidentally breaking a neighbor's window or sometimes push the limits with those who just might not recognize his future worldwide fame.

Practice was relentless . . . against a tree, through a knothole on the barn, anywhere but old Dandy's rump. Deep in the woods, he could emulate what he imagined to be the throwing styles of the big leaguers. He skipped flat rocks on the stream, gathered round ones for hitting squirrels, blackbirds, and sparrows.

"Many a bagful of game I got with stones," he would claim.

He could also brag about his prowess at checkers, even taking his board down to the swimming hole. Didn't matter the age of his competition, he was game.

In 1890, Christy became "second catcher" for the town's amateur baseball team, a glamorous title for a water boy who essentially chased foul balls for free. He loved it.

"I became a known factor in the baseball circles of Factoryville," Christy would later write, "and might be said to have started my career."

The Factoryville pitcher taught him the art of throwing curves.

"After considerable practice, I managed to curve the ball, but I never knew where it was going."

At the same time, he was growing so fast that he earned the nickname "Husk" from the older boys, who still ordered him to right field when he regularly invaded their ballgames. Husk was a bit clumsy and less than sterling in the field.

"I was pretty good at chasing after the balls that got away from me," Christy kidded. "And I could throw hard and straight."

He was not, however, particularly good at hitting, holding to a cross-handed batting style he had probably picked up from hoeing the field.

"Once in a while, I would connect with the ball and it would always be a long wallop, because I was a big, husky, country boy; but more often I ignominiously struck out. My real baseball start was not very auspicious."

When Jane Stoughton was 10 years old, she had never heard of Factoryville. Jenny, as she was often called, had been born on January 9, 1880 in Millersburg, a small borough on the Susquehanna River. In 1898, the family moved 40 miles north to the borough of Lewisburg, resting 100 miles southwest of Christy's home.

Buying a two-story brick home at 129 Market Street, Frank and Julia Stoughton took care that their five girls and two boys regularly read the bible, the family attending the Presbyterian Church just down the block near the river. They also advocated a strong awareness of current events. Jenny, the second oldest, already knew about Thomas Edison's Electric Illuminating Company, George Eastman's portable camera, the surrender of Geronimo, and the Great Johnstown Flood of 1889 that killed 2,209 people in western Pennsylvania.

Jenny had enjoyed reading from an early age, her bookshelf filled with the *Elsie Dinsmore* stories by Martha Finley and *Little Women* by Louisa May Alcott. She also loved the fresh air and playing with friends – Fox and Hounds, Hide and Seek, Ox in the Ditch. And while she sometimes played catch, she did not know that the Brooklyn Bridegrooms were the best team in baseball or that Oyster Burns led the National League with 13 homers and 128 RBIs.

Even if she did care, Jenny would certainly not discuss baseball lingo with her father. Frank Stoughton was the superintendent of the L & T Railroad, an 80-mile east-west line between Lewisburg and Tyrone. He worked hard and earned a lucrative salary. He thought baseball was stupid.

In mid-summer of 1894, Christy Mathewson would land his first appearance on center stage when the Factoryville club found itself temporarily without its only two twirlers. After the team captain learned that young Husk could throw, an emergency Saturday morning tryout was organized right in the middle of Main Street. The audition was witnessed by most of the town, the older citizens shaking their heads in dismay that a 14-year-old boy could be even considered to pitch against adults. The entire Factoryville team stepped up to take their swings.

"I put everything I had on the ball," recalled Christy of the two-hour tryout. "When I struck out the team captain, he slapped me on the back and said, 'you'll do.'"

That afternoon, seven miles down the road in Mill City, Factoryville and its young pitcher would prevail 19-17. And even though he would also knock in the eventual winning runs with a bases-loaded hit that sailed over the leftfielder's head, what remained sharpest in Christy's memory was the look of his envious friends, standing numb as he rode out of Factoryville on a horse-drawn wagon to play baseball with the men. Christy would long claim that one Saturday in the summer of '94 as his "proudest day."

Baseball was fun, but nothing was more important in the Mathewson household than religion and education. All of the children had chores on the small farm, all enjoyed the challenge of learning, and no one ever missed a Sunday at the First Baptist Church, listening as Pastor John Howard Harris spoke of the strong and moral will, of always doing the right thing, of never wavering from simple goodness.

"Honesty, because it is essentially mighty, needs no hiding," said Pastor Harris. "It is the moral and spiritual developments that distinguish the complete man."

Christy and his family greatly admired their preacher. He was energetic, physically fit, a dynamic orator who mixed a powerful intellect with a resounding faith.

The same age as Christy's father, Harris had also been a teenager in the Civil War, fighting at Richmond and Lynchburg with Company H of the 206th Pennsylvania Volunteers. After graduating from the University at Lewisburg in 1869 (now Bucknell), Harris was a founder and the first principal of the Keystone Academy, also teaching Greek and German.

The only high school between Scranton and the New York border, Keystone Academy was housed in a modern four-story building in Factoryville. When Christy was born in 1880, Harris was both head of the academy and the pastor of the Baptist Church.

By the time Christy reached high school, Pastor Harris was no longer with Keystone, but his philosophy had definitely made an impression with the youngster – strong body, energetic mind, and unwavering principles. An outstanding student, Christy also excelled in football, basketball, and baseball.

In August 1897, after Factoryville had finished its baseball schedule, the Mathewson' home was visited by the coach of Mill City. Since Christy still had more than a month before starting his senior year at Keystone, why not throw for Mill City? They would even pay him a dollar per game.

Christy was shocked, amazed.

"It was such fun for me to play ball that the idea of getting paid for it struck me as finding money."

The new Factoryville ace would bring his own catcher, Fred Brauer. They would meet halfway on the "lower road" to Mill City and share the loot on their way back home.

But Mill City was just the beginning of the gold rush. After beginning the summer of '98 twirling for the Scranton YMCA, Christy was offered $20 a month (plus board) by the Honesdale Eagles, a strong semipro team that would win the Wayne County League championship.

Thanks to the opulent payday, Christy didn't mind being 35 miles from Factoryville.

"It looked good to me," he said, "because I knew I would need all the money I could save for college."

If only he could make money playing football?

The early word was that Christy, a powerful runner and exceptional kicker, would take his football talents to the University of Pennsylvania. The Quakers were the defending national champs, having finished 15-0 in 1897. Their returning All-America tackle, John Outland, would be captain and running back on the '98 squad.

Christy would have undoubtedly made a great addition to the Quakers. Instead, he selected Bucknell University, where he made a modest impact his freshman season with a couple of touchdowns and field goals as the Bison went 4-4-3.

Meanwhile, Penn would win its first nine games in '98 by a combined score of 356-0, Outland a repeat All-America. As a sidebar, the Quakers played all but one of their games at Franklin Field. The team finished 12-1, its only loss on the road at Harvard.

For a time, Christy considered delaying college and entering the military. In February 1898, he was a senior at Keystone Academy when the U.S.S. Maine – America's newest battleship – was sunk in Havana Harbor, killing 260 sailors. With daily reports of the Spanish-American War, Christy was enthralled by the exploits of Admiral George Dewey at Manila Bay and Colonel Teddy Roosevelt leading the volunteer Rough Riders up San Juan Hill. It would be a short war, Spain's colonial rule in the Americas and western Pacific erased by August.

Christy headed to college, pleased that the United States was rapidly becoming a world power and giving no second thoughts to attending Penn. For him, Bucknell was perfect.

CHAPTER TWO

A small college noted for its disciplined academics, Bucknell was located smack dab in the middle of Pennsylvania. It was a gorgeous campus with stately brick buildings sitting high above the Susquehanna River. Originally known as the University at Lewisburg, it was founded by Baptists in 1856 with its name changed in 1886 in recognition of a robust gift from William Bucknell. While the school maintained Christian principles, enrollment was open to all religions, which was only one of its progressive attributes . . . Bucknell also admitted women.

But it wasn't women that attracted Christy to the college. First glimpse and he knew that this was where he belonged. Plus, a good friend of the family was already there.

In late September 1898, Christy was standing at the Scranton Train Depot when he ran into Frank Stanton, who was also headed to Bucknell for early football practice. While Stanton had graduated from the Peddie School in Hightstown, New Jersey, he had actually met Christy three years earlier at a baseball game.

When the two arrived at Milton, they caught a carriage and crossed the river to Lewisburg. Christy had just turned 18, one of the youngest members in the Class of 1902. At a time when barely six percent of Americans even graduated from high school, Bucknell was welcoming 75 new students, the largest first-year class in school history. College wasn't cheap. Tuition, room, and board added up to $140 per year, plus 25 cents per week for anyone wishing laundry services.

Although shy, Christy was never lost in the crowd. He was tall and strikingly handsome with chiseled muscles signaling that he could run as fast as he could factor equations. And, goodness, was he smart. His first semester, he steeped himself in algebra, trigonometry, geometry, French, German, and Latin. He blazed through the school's required reading list – *Paradise Lost, Last of the Mohigans, Silas Marner, House of the Seven Gables, Ivanhoe, and Macbeth.* Most of his grades hovered around 95 with his lowest a 90 . . . if only he had hit the Latin a bit harder.

Christy was the only male student from Factoryville, although he had gone to the Keystone Academy with his good friend and new roommate, Ernest Sterling. First on Christy's agenda, after reporting to the football coach, was to look up his childhood pastor. John Howard Harris had been president of Bucknell since 1889. A strong advocate of Christian education, Harris would serve as Bucknell's president for 30 years.

Gilbert and Nervy were thrilled. John Harris would be the perfect guide for their son's education. Christy's baseball craze would finally be replaced by a quest for a real career.

"I thought baseball would last a little while," Minerva would later write, "and that then my hope of his being a preacher would be realized."

Christy's parents were absolutely correct about the impact President Harris would have on their son. Christy was a regular guest at the President's House, stationed right across the street from Loomis Field. Mrs. Harris, the former Lucy Bailey, had also grown up in Factoryville. She was deeply involved in church, charity, and the temperance movement.

His first Sunday on campus, Christy was invited to dinner by President and Mrs. Harris. Frank Stanton also received an after-church invitation.

"We were dressed in our best," said Stanton. "They really made us feel at home."

Stanton got a kick out of President Harris telling a story about the old days at the Factoryville church.

"He recalled Christy at the age of eight sitting in the front seat, very straight, with well-combed hair and a white collar, paying strict attention," said Stanton. "The doctor seemed to think it was a bit unusual."

Well, Christy always took his faith seriously . . . a trait that would never change.

Actually, religion was a key element of a Bucknell education at the turn of the century. Each morning, a required religious service was held at Bucknell Hall with President Harris often preaching the sermon. Afternoon and evening services were "urged, but not required." On Sundays, the 269 Bucknell students had to attend a church of their choice in Lewisburg.

As he had done from the pulpit in Factoryville, President Harris had plenty of advice for young Mathewson and his fellow students, centering on complete moral action.

"The student must aim at the highest manhood," he stressed, "act from the highest motive, and pursue right ends by right means."

To Christy, these words simply reiterated the thought process and values he had followed all his life.

"Energy of will is developed by right doing," said Harris. "Idleness debilitates the will; vice rots it out."

Well, Christy Mathewson was never one to be idle. With an intelligence and curiosity that was constantly ignited by a fierce inner drive, he loved the school, the work, the challenge, and the people. He immersed himself in academics, athletics, and social activities. He would star in three sports. He played bass horn in the Bucknell band, joined Phi Gamma Delta fraternity, was inducted into two prestigious literary societies and a leadership club. As a freshman, he was the class historian, showing a flare for writing that was both humorous and noble.

In the Bucknell yearbook, *L'Agenda,* he wrote about the first-year students riding sleighs through the snow of downtown Lewisburg while giving their "class yell in open defiance of the chagrined sophomores." Although the sophomores (Class of 1901) were outnumbered, 75-54, they still attempted to impose their standing over the younger students. Christy reported that there came a time to give the sophomores "a needed lesson."

"One morning," he wrote, "we overtook the sophs, who were hastening from chapel, and we proceeded to roll them about in the snow. It was a shame to so misuse the pure, clean snow, but it left the defeated sophs with cleaner faces and a clearer perception of right and wrong."

Another lesson that every Bucknellian soon learned was that "Rubber Leg" was as good at games of the mind as he was on the athletic fields . . . no one could dent his skill at cards, chess, or especially checkers. The yearbook duly noted that when Mr. Mathewson left campus for the fields of professional baseball, he forgot several items in his dorm room – "three decks of cards and a box of chips."

By his third year at Bucknell, Christy was elected class president, served on the Junior Ball Committee, never missed a class or assignment, and remained an "A" student . . . except for that horrid 75 in geology . . . just about the time he was falling deeply in love with Jenny Stoughton.

Thanks to yet another influence from Factoryville, Christy also participated in drama and poetry. Lincoln Hulley, one of Bucknell's young and dynamic professors, had graduated from Keystone Academy 15 years earlier. A history professor with degrees from Bucknell and Harvard, Hulley was also a talented playwright and poet. In 1904, he would become president of Stetson University in Florida, a post he would hold for three decades.

While Christy would play three sports at Bucknell, baseball was his least productive. As a freshman, he was immediately christened the captain and star hurler of a fairly terrible team.

"No pitcher can win games when his men don't field well behind him, or when they refuse to bat in any runs," said Christy, ever one to be honest or painfully blunt.

The spring of '99 would be the only time he played baseball at Bucknell . . . and it nearly proved to be his last year of baseball anywhere.

CHAPTER THREE

Summer 1899 . . . Portland, Maine

No outs, bases loaded, bottom of the eighth inning. The Portland Phenoms – runaway leaders of the Class F New England League – were about to enhance their 7-0 pounding of the last-place Taunton Herrings.

Phenomenal Smith – the Portland manager, left fielder, and star hitter – sat in the dugout, hands rubbing against the handle of his bat; eyes focused on the opposing pitcher . . . every twitch, every movement. The twirler was tall, muscular, and quite young.

"How old you think that kid is, Stubby?" Phenom John blurted to James "Stub" Smith, no relation.

"I heard he was 18," answered Stub, "some college kid from Pennsylvania, I think."

"He's a big kid," said the manager. "He's got some talent."

"Phenom, we're killing him," giggled Stub.

"No, we're killing his stupid team, Stubby. Look at this kid. He's in the box firin' away like it's a tie game in the ninth, actin' like it's fun to be behind by seven runs . . . maybe he can't add."

The Smith boys chuckled.

"Strike three," the umpire bellowed as Taunton's young pitcher, Christy Mathewson, sliced the corner of the plate for the first out of the inning.

Phenom would have disputed the call, but he was still chuckling about his college-kid-can't-add joke. Besides, the bases were still loaded.

"Yeah Stub," said Phenom, "I'm thinkin' this Mathewson kid is gonna be a pretty fair twirler someday."

"Well, you know your talent, Phenom," said Stubby. "Look who you got at shortstop."

Phenom smiled as he popped the head of his bat on the dirt.

"Well Stubby, I'm on deck. I sure do hope the kid throws me another one of those roundhouse curves so I can clear the bases."

Phenom was already two-for-three against Mathewson with a sacrifice fly to boot. His hits were the direct results of two slow curves; both religiously delivered after two strikes.

But now there were two outs as Mathewson fooled George Noblitt into popping out to the Taunton first baseman, Buster Burrell, who had managed to make a routine fly into an adventure.

Phenom stepped to the plate, pretending that his 34-year-old body didn't hurt that much, that agility would be his forever. It may have looked a mismatch, the gigantic Mathewson at 6-foot-2 and the pudgy left-handed hitter a generous 5-foot-6. But 15 years of experience certainly favored Phenom, a feared clutch hitter who was batting near .400 for the season.

"Bases loaded," he whispered to himself as he dug his spikes into the now soft dirt.

From the box, Matty seemed unfazed, slowly beginning his big and easy windup, delivering a fastball to the outside corner, not worthy of a swing, but close enough for the umpire – standing behind the pitcher – to call a strike.

Phenomenal figured Mathewson would try the outside fastball once again . . . he guessed right, but lined it just foul of first . . . Burrell barely moved.

"Give it a rip, Phenom," someone yelled from the big crowd of several hundred Portland fans.

Phenom John smiled as he backed away from home to stretch his neck and take a couple of practice swings. Now, he had the kid for certain. It would be a two-strike, chest-high curve . . . guaranteed . . .

"Like a knife to an orange," Phenom mumbled to himself, "cut it in two."

He even had visions of taking it to the fence, although the ball was in pretty bad shape . . . looking more like a dark and scuffed onion after eight innings of abuse.

The Portland runners took their leads as Mathewson gave Smith the "try-hitting-this-one" look. Phenom returned the gesture with a gritty "bring-it-on" smirk, knowing full well what the kid was planning.

Mathewson delivered . . . sure enough . . . inside . . . chest high . . . Phenom held his stride . . . waiting as the ball began its break . . . except it didn't curve . . . and his swing was late . . . a fastball?

"Strike three" came the call as Phenom completely missed . . . outwitted by a college kid . . . who was supposed to throw a curve.

Squeezing his bat and bulging his eyes, Phenom John grumbled toward the dugout, having his glove tossed toward him by Stub Smith.

"You're right," said Stub. "The kid is good."

The Portland Phenoms would finish 60-41 in 1899, easily capturing the New England title. Phenom John would hit .382, not bad for a former big league twirler.

John Smith had spent eight years in the majors, beginning in '84 with the Philadelphia Athletics of the American Association. He would notch a 54-74 career major-league record, his best season in 1887 when he won 25 games for Baltimore (and lost 30). He earned the "Phenomenal" nickname early in his profession when he struck out 16 batters in a game without the ball once leaving the infield. Now, the glory days behind him, he was having great success as a minor-league outfielder and coach.

By the time he would retire, Phenom John would log 20 years as a player and 11 as a manager. His teams would earn six pennants.

When James "Stub" Smith landed in Portland, he had only been playing professional baseball for one season and seemed to be heading in the wrong direction. He began his rookie year as the 24-year-old shortstop of the Class B Fall River Indians before getting called up by the Boston Beaneaters of the National League. He did not fare well, dinking a lone single in 10 attempts, unceremoniously released after three games. Figuring he'd be back with the Beaneaters with a bit more experience, he started the '99 season with the Worcester Farmers of the Class A Eastern League, but was quickly dropped to Class F Portland. Stub would play nine years of pro ball, but never return to the majors.

Meanwhile, the summer of '99 in Taunton was a disaster for 18-year-old Christy Mathewson, stuck on a nine that finished deep in the New England cellar. He had started the season happily earning a rent-free

$20 per month at Honesdale, leaving in mid-July for nearly five times the salary to play in the New England League. Heading for another title, Honesdale hated losing its best twirler. On July 16, the *Wayne Independent* wrote that Christy was "a young man of good habits and we expect to hear well of him in Massachusetts."

Instructed to meet the Herrings in Manchester, Christy stopped in Boston to witness his first major-league game, Cy Young pitching for the Beaneaters against Kid Nichols of the Cleveland Spiders. Boston would win.

On July 21, before 200 rooters at Manchester, Christy lost the first game of his minor-league career, 6-5. It would not get much better for the Taunton Herrings. The hitting was bad and fielding worse. The college kid started 15 games and completed them all, but ended with a dismal 2-13 record, the scourge of a shabby defense.

"This team makes enough errors of commission and omission to send it to Hades," Christy wrote in a letter back home. "I pitched in one game where we had 10 errors, beside half a dozen passed balls by the catcher who does not seem able to hold me."

At least Matty fared better than the other Herring hurler, Tom Brady, who would yield 137 runs in 120 innings while going 2-11. It would be Brady's third and last year in professional baseball.

To make matters worse, the Herrings could not attract fans nor keep up with the payroll, the owner continually promising his players that the money was on the way. It was not going to happen. In early September, the club went out of business, leaving the players to complete the final road game on their own. On Labor Day, the newly defunct Herrings lost a triple-header at Newport, Rhode Island.

"It was sort of a benefit game for the players so that we could get back to our homes," said Christy. "If it had rained, I guess we would have had to walk."

Christy had been drawn to Massachusetts with an attractive $90 per month contract and, seven weeks later, was owed more than $200 by the Herrings . . . he got nothing.

Well, he did finally learn how to bat properly, having grown tired of fans and opponents poking fun at his "country-boy" swing. It was tough to break the old cross-handed habit, but he managed to hit .232, which actually was one of the team's better batting averages.

He also, when not pitching, got to spend quality time practicing his dropkicking. In fact, Christy's sideline football exhibitions were often more spectacular than the baseball games.

However, what would prove to be the most important benefit of Christy's horrible summer of '99 was that he would learn a strange new pitch from a journeyman lefty, William Kershaw. During practice one day, Kershaw showed young Christy his freak pitch, sort of an against-the-grain curve that crashed in on batters rather than away from them. It was not only unique, but near impossible to hit.

"He could throw it," said Christy, "but had absolutely no control over where it would go."

In his final season of a short two-year professional career, Kershaw did not win a game for Taunton, nor was he ever paid.

To Christy's mind, Kershaw's freak pitch was crafty, but would probably never work. Still, he felt it was worth practicing, even if he didn't throw it in a game. And he already had his fastball, roundhouse curve, and surprise drop.

When an emotionally burned Matty returned home to Factoryville for a few days, he was thinking that perhaps baseball might not be worth the effort, bad lessons having continually sapped the fun.

"I felt rather discouraged," he said. "My summer had been a financial failure and baseball prospects were none too bright."

Thank goodness he was heading back to Bucknell to study hard and play a real sport . . . football.

Bucknell's Loomis Field.

It should be noted that it was legal for athletes to play baseball for pay during the summer and still participate in college athletics. It also should be realized that baseball was essentially the only professional team sport at the time. Had there been a professional football league even approaching the scope of baseball, Christy Mathewson might have followed a different path. Even more, what pigskin glory might he have achieved if the forward pass had existed at the turn of the century? Matty no doubt would have been the nation's greatest quarterback.

"I'd rather play one good game of football than a dozen games of baseball," he said. "I never drew the thrill nor the pleasure I used to get in a moleskin suit while hitting a line or taking a shot at a field goal in a tight pinch."

His college sweetheart agreed.

"This may sound strange," said Jane, "but I never saw him play baseball until he joined the Giants. I saw him play plenty of football and I believe he was a greater football player than baseball. He could do everything."

Essentially, Christy thrived with the season.

Football in the fall and early winter ignited the vigor within his soul. To Christy, the sport was a beautiful concoction of vitality and violence, tactics and camaraderie, running full force through the wind with the power to hit and the strength to endure . . . an entire team working and moving as one . . . limps and bruises becoming the medals of a glorious battle.

Of course, with the ice and snow of winter, basketball took its turn. It was quick and vigorous with the sound of leather on hardwood and the steamy sweat of the indoor gym. Then again, basketball didn't have the tradition or glamour of his other two favorites. Well, it had only been around since 1891.

With the spring and summer, Matty became obsessed with the splendor of playing baseball. The dirt and sweat of a long, hot afternoon charged the essence of his body and mind. Within the pitcher's box, he possessed a passion to outwit every hitter, conquer every dilemma, and win every game. Arguments might rage, he simply watched . . . let's play some baseball.

With Matty, the key was competition. Athletics, cards, checkers, puzzles . . . he played to win . . . but only by his own prowess and skills . . . never by deceit . . . always fair, always honest . . . any other way would be against the grain of his character.

CHAPTER FOUR

October 4, 1899 . . . Philadelphia

Christy sat comfortably in the hotel lobby, reading the Philadelphia Inquirer. After two easy victories to start the season, the Bison football' team had taken a train to Philly the previous day and were now well rested for the sure slaughter that was scheduled that afternoon at Franklin Field.

"Christy Mathewson," he heard from an approaching voice.

Christy looked up from the paper, immediately realizing that he knew the visitor . . . from somewhere.

"Phenom John Smith," the man said as he extended his hand.

Christy smiled and stood to return the handshake.

"Yes, from Portland," he said, now realizing that he towered over the legendary Phenom. "Please, have a seat. You sure clubbed me for some good hits over the summer."

"And you got me as well," said Phenom John. "I'll never forget that two-out, bases-loaded curve you never threw me."

"I won't either," said Christy with a sly smile.

"I know you have a big football game today," said Phenom, "but I was wondering if we might talk a moment about baseball."

"I have to be honest that baseball is a pretty far distance from my mind right now," said Christy. "I didn't have the greatest experience at Taunton."

"No, I understand," said Phenom. "I do want you to know that I believe you have incredible pitching potential. I'm moving up to the

Virginia League this season to coach in Norfolk. I'm here to offer you a contract."

Christy wanted to appear hesitant, but surprised even himself at his sudden interest, as if the refreshed idea of "good and fun" baseball had miraculously dissolved the memory of old disappointments.

"I do love to pitch," said Christy.

"I know you do," replied Phenom, placing an official looking paper between them. "I'd like to offer you a contract for $80 a month pitching for Norfolk."

Christy seemed momentarily baffled . . .

"I made $90 a month last year for Taunton," he said.

"That's fine," said Phenom, "but they didn't pay you. We will actually pay you real money to pitch for us."

Christy thought deeply. He didn't have anything else planned for next summer.

"Sure," he said, looking his new manager squarely in the eye.

"Wonderful," said Phenom, handing the contract and a pen to Christy.

Christy glanced through the short contract with clauses that prohibited drinking, swearing, and embarrassing the club.

"I've heard great things about you, Mr. Smith," said Matty.

"Please, call me John or Phenom," said the manager with a personable grin. "Some folks still call me Phenomenal."

Both laughed as Christy signed his name.

"Wonderful," said Phenom. "I'm excited about next season. We're putting together a really fine team and I've got big plans for you."

"Great," said Christy.

"Look, I've got tickets for this afternoon's game," said Phenom as he rose from the chair. "I was born and raised right here in Philly, but I'll be the guy cheering for Bucknell."

"Thanks," said Christy, laughingly pointing his finger at Phenom's chest. "Tell the Quakers that the Bison will not be taking any prisoners today."

"Yep, bad news for Old Penn," chuckled Phenom as he placed his copy of the contract in his coat pocket.

Christy smiled, once again feeling wealthy.

John Smith would run into another baseball manager that day at Franklin Field, Connie Mack of the Philadelphia Athletics. Smith pointed out the "husky young chap" he had just signed and told Mack that Mathewson was a definite major-league prospect.

For historical accuracy, the Penn Quakers were not worried about Christy or the Bucknell Bison.

The University of Pennsylvania had suffered only two losses in its past 71 games. The Quakers played in one of the best stadiums in the country and seldom allowed an opponent to even score. John Outland may have graduated, but "Old Penn" had crushed its first two opponents of the '99 season by a 76-0 margin. It was expected by all Philadelphians that the upcoming encounter with the Orange and Blue of Bucknell would be no different.

Founded in 1740, Penn was the fourth college on American soil, the first university. Its sports venue, Franklin Field, was built in 1895 on the eastern edge of campus, separated from downtown Philly by the Schuylkill River. The site of the Penn Relays, the $100,000 stadium was a marvel of modernity, seating nearly 20,000 fans.

Unlike most playing fields of the time, Franklin Field had an actual scoreboard, which – on October 3, 1899 – must have looked quite strange to the hometown crowd. At halftime, Penn had but 11 points and the visitors 10, Christy Mathewson having nailed a pair of drop kicks from 25 and 30 yards out. It was 20 minutes, according to the next day's *New York Times,* that "startled the football world."

"The kicking of Mathewson," the *Times* proclaimed, "was the finest seen here in a long time."

Before heading to the locker room to recharge his Quakers, Penn coach George Woodruff first lambasted the officiating. At the half, according to the newspaper, "Penn protested against the partiality shown by G.W. Hoskins of State College and who, by the way, is Bucknell's coach."

Yes, in his first year with the Bison, George Hoskins was also the umpire that day, having accepted the appointment to officiate before taking the coaching position in Lewisburg. Hoskins should have known he would be recognized in Philadelphia. In 1892, he was the first Penn State football coach, his teams compiling a 17-4-4 record over four seasons, three of those losses occurring at Penn. An accomplished trainer,

"Doc" Hoskins also had coached football at Pitt before moving to Bucknell.

But now he found himself in the middle of a vehement controversy, finally agreeing to switch positions with the other official. John Minds of Philadelphia became the umpire and Hoskins the referee, a spot where he could apparently do less damage with his whistle.

A more powerful change, however, would be the attitude of the Quakers, who blazed for 36 unanswered points to win 47-10.

The *Times* made clear that the "Pennsylvania protest does not detract from the brilliant work of Mathewson."

As for Bucknell's coach, he had to sneak out of the stadium under the protection of his players. And, despite the dual earnings for both coaching and officiating, Hoskins actually lost money, having promised as motivation that the first player to score against Penn would receive a brand new $7 pair of shoes and a second score would be worth a new raincoat. Mathewson won both prizes.

Plus, when the Bison arrived back at the hotel, Phenom John Smith was waiting in the lobby. The new Norfolk manager pulled out the baseball contract, drawing a line through the original financial promise.

"That was a swell game this afternoon," he said to Matty, "and because I liked the way in which you kicked those two field goals, I'm going to make your salary $90 instead of $80."

The 1899 Bison football team finished 6-4 on the season. Christy accumulated seven touchdowns and six field goals, including two long drop kicks in a pair of 5-0 victories over Lehigh and Penn State. As for punting, "Mathewson gained 15 to 20 yards on every exchange," reported Bucknell's student newspaper, the *Orange and Blue.*

The sophomore was not the superstar in basketball, but did play a commendable center. Bucknell was near unbeatable at home, Tustin Gym featuring a short indoor track that circled the court but trimmed the corners of the baseline to create a slick advantage. Overall, the Bison finished 6-3 with victories over Penn State and Cornell. They did, however, lose to the Pittston YMCA.

CHAPTER FOUR

At the beginning of the new century, the United States was officially a world military power and industrial giant, producing half the earth's oil and a third of its steel.

While most of the 75 million Americans still relied on the horse and buggy for transportation, profound changes were occurring, from the light bulb and telephone to the automobile and beyond.

Out west, Utah was the nation's 45th state and Hawaii would soon be annexed. With roughly 102,000 residents, Los Angeles was the same size as Scranton. And New York City (population 3.5 million) was bigger than Chicago and Philadelphia combined.

Certainly, all was not ideal in America – racism was rampant, wealth was unbalanced, working conditions were often harsh, more than a quarter of a million children worked in mines, and one in seven Americans died of tuberculosis.

Still, in its final editorial of 1899, the *New York Times* predicted that the new century would be "a brighter dawn for human civilization."

In the spring of 1900, refusing an onslaught of requests to play baseball for the Bison, Christy wrapped up his second year at Bucknell with another solid academic performance and headed south to Norfolk.

Christy's debut was shaky, walking the bases loaded to start the game, then giving up a triple as the Norfolk fans hooted for Phenom to yank the youngster. All told, the 19-year-old allowed five runs in the top of the first.

"I was nervous when I went into the box," said Christy. "Somehow I couldn't locate the plate."

He then hurled eight shutout innings as Norfolk came from behind for a 6-5 victory. Phenom John was right about the value of that extra $10 a month he promised the young collegiate hurler as Christy would lead the Phenoms to the Virginia League title with a blistering 20-2 record that included a 12-inning 1-0 loss to Hampton. Christy notched four shutouts and a no-hitter. But, really, how could they lose? They had Phenom John in left and Stubby Smith at short. In fact, the no-hit game on June 12 was scoreless into the bottom of the ninth when Stubby doubled and Phenom drove him home with the winner.

Like all minor-league clubs at the time, the Phenoms were constantly searching for revenue . . . and Christy Mathewson was suddenly a hot commodity. When both the Philadelphia Athletics and New York Giants offered Norfolk $2,000 to purchase Mathewson's contract, Phenom John gave Matty the choice of where he would like to pitch.

"At first I wanted to go to Philadelphia, because it was closer to my home," said Matty, "but after studying the pitching staffs of both clubs, I decided that the opportunity in New York was better."

The deal sending Matty to the majors was struck, his salary to remain at $90 per month with the understanding that he would be returned to Norfolk if he "failed to make good."

Matty reported to the Polo Grounds in mid-July of 1900, George Davis greeting the rookie for a round of batting practice. Davis, an outstanding shortstop and new manager of the Giants, was exactly a decade older than Christy. He also was a community hero, three months earlier having helped save the lives of two women and a child from a burning building.

Davis, who would someday be elected to the Baseball Hall of Fame, took an immediate liking to the rookie. He was impressed with the fastball, then hit Christy's roundhouse curve out of the park.

"Put that in cold storage," he yelled to the pitcher's box. "That ain't any good in this company. A man with paralysis in both arms could get himself set in time to hit that one. You got anything else?"

Christy threw the drop ball.

"Now, that's what we call a curve ball in the Big Leagues," Davis hollered. "Got anything else?"

What followed was a dose of good fortune as Christy decided to try his freak pitch. Davis never had a chance against the surprising outside-in break and missed connecting by about a foot. Christy would later write that he would "never forget how Davis' eyes bulged."

"What was that?" bellowed the manager, "I've never seen that before."

"That's one I picked up, but never use," Christy said. "It's kind of a freak ball."

"Throw it again."

This time Davis knew what was coming and still couldn't hit it.

"That's a good one," he yelled. "Sort of a fallaway or fadeaway."

Davis was delighted, instructing his young pitcher to work on the pitch until it was mastered.

"And there," Christy would later write, "in the morning practice at the Polo Grounds in 1900, the *fadeaway* was born and christened by George Davis. He called some left-handers to bat against it. Nearly all of them missed it and were loud in their praise."

Packed house at the Polo Grounds.

In mid-July, New York City was hit by a killer heat wave that would take 39 lives, including 33 children under the age of five.

On the afternoon of July 17, the third straight day with temperatures in the high 90s, Christy Mathewson made his major-league debut at Brooklyn's Washington Park, relieving Ed Doheny in the fifth inning against the first-place Superbas. Before the game, Manager Davis told sportswriter John B. Foster that the new pitcher "may be wild, but somehow he looks good to me."

For the record, Matty's first major-league pitch was a ball, outside and high. In four innings, he would hit three batters, walk two, and allow six runs.

The good news was that the rookie got to swing a bat. The bad news was that he had to face Joe "Iron Man" McGinnity, the National League's top twirler on his way to a 28-8 record.

"I figured that when I came to bat, I would open their eyes," said Matty. "Down at Norfolk, I had played in the outfield when not pitching and I considered myself a great hitter. I went up to the plate and McGinnity threw me one of those underhanded upshots. I nearly broke my back trying to connect with it. All told, he threw me three of those balls and I then walked back to the bench with my bat in my hand and my heart in my throat."

Iron Man McGinnity, who would one day be Christy's teammate, would cruise to victory that day. And although Doheny was tagged with the loss, some of the veteran players on the club loudly ridiculed Christy's performance.

Beyond the stench of last place, there were problems in the Giants' dugout. Davis was quite friendly, as was catcher Frank Bowerman, but few players even bothered to recognize the youngster, quickly branding him an aloof "college pinhead." An aggravated Matty did not even attempt to ease the tension, stubbornly removing himself to the far end of the bench and ignoring all of them.

He certainly didn't gain any new friendships after his second appearance in relief on July 25, once again tagged for six runs. On August 4, Matty relieved in the seventh with a one-run lead over St. Louis, but the Cardinals' feisty third-sacker, John McGraw, would score the winning run and hand Matty his first major-league loss. It was an entire month before Mathewson would pitch again, actually starting a game on September 6 against the Chicago Orphans. Matty went the distance, but lost 6-5 due to an error by Jack Doyle that led to four runs in the first inning. Two weeks later, after a stinging loss in relief at Boston's South End Downs, Christy's 0-3 mark earned him a disappointing boot back to Norfolk.

It would be an interesting winter . . .

CHAPTER FIVE

October 1900 . . . Lewisburg

Christy sat nervously in the living room of the Stoughton' home. He had dressed formally for a Sunday afternoon visit, a dark blue suit with white starched collar that jutted high on his neck. Although the attire was quite fashionable, he nevertheless felt a touch choked.

Jane, as always, was beautiful, wearing a full-length dress with a modest light blue pattern. She too was probably somewhat overdressed, but being with Christy was special . . . she had no qualms about looking good.

"Christy, when you go back to baseball this summer," she said in a slow and deep voice. "I hope you might find time to write."

He tried to look into her eyes, but could not bust his awkward shyness. He was the greatest drop kicker in the world; no matter the angle or the mud . . . Walter Camp had said so. And from the pitcher's box, he could strike out the side with the bases loaded in a foreign town with evil rooters in the stands . . . and never even sweat. But courting was a disaster . . . his stomach was in shambles, his nerves over the fence, his voice seemed invariably high pitched with chatter that bounced from being silly to uncontrollably stupid. Jane considered his shyness charming, sensing that his real personality was simply hiding, that a strong man definitely existed beneath this schoolboy wreck. Plus, he was unbelievably handsome.

"I'll write all the time," Christy answered, somehow able to speak an entire sentence without an error.

"I'd love that," she said, blushing that she had actually used such a forward word as *love*.

Christy's smile nearly popped off his face. What should he say now?

Pulling at his tightening collar, he quickly glanced around the room... no sisters, no brothers, no mother . . . and, thank goodness, no father. Ever so slowly, Christy leaned forward and put his slightly shaking pitching fingers on Jane's hand. She smiled while soothingly covering his hand within hers . . . he gulped.

Like a bolt of lightning, the front door blew open, Jane's younger brother, Gus, charging into the room. Christy's hand jumped, but Jane pulled it back.

Gus bolted past, not even slowing to look.

Christy was always a sharp dresser.

It had been most unorthodox how the two college sweethearts had met. Both Jane and her cousin, Louise Albright, attended Bucknell's Female Institute. Extremely shy and proper, Louise had been seriously dating Christy for more than a year. While she adored his good looks and intelligence, she did not see a future with a baseball player, nor did she grasp his sense of humor. When Christy asked if she would consider marrying him, Louise flatly said "no" . . . but she did know someone who would be perfect for him.

Jane had actually been engaged for a short period of time to Harvey Marsh, Bucknell Class of 1897, but had already broken it off before Louise introduced her to Christy.

The two enjoyed walks by shore of the Susquehanna or through the heart of the lovely Victorian town. Jane was stunned that this wonderfully polite and athletic man actually knew the name of every tree and flower. They shared thoughts on literature, faith, and sometimes baseball. And, yes, both agreed that women should have the right to vote. They shared quick wit, intelligence, manners; a way with the world that the other adored . . . and it was not long before they were discussing future dreams.

Although marriage was soon understood, they both professed it was important to first be financially sound. Jane was 21 years old and Christy half a year younger. He wanted to make money pitching baseballs and her father disapproved. She sensed that all of the obstacles would eventually crumble . . . and she was right.

After Christy's junior football season, he starred for a dynamic basketball five that finished 12-1, including victories over Penn 32-9 and Gettysburg 54-11. Although the Orange and Blue averaged more than 26 points a game, the highest in the six-year history of the sport at Bucknell, the team turned cold on a February night at Williamsport, losing 8-5.

While Christy was locked in school and romance, his worth as a baseball player was being appraised. Preparing for its inaugural major-league season, the upstart American League would be based on honest organization, good sportsmanship, and stadiums that would be safe for women and children . . . a world away from the brand of hooligan ball that had long scarred the National League.

Born with a wandering eye for New York City, the Americans immediately went head-to-head with franchises in Chicago, Boston, and Philadelphia. Its other markets were Baltimore, Detroit, Milwaukee, Cleveland, and Washington D.C.

The American League would sign 82 players from the senior circuit, including Christy Mathewson by the Philadelphia Athletics. Fresh from signing Nap Lajoie away from the cross-town NL Phillies, manager Connie Mack offered Christy a contract for the 1901 season. A man of high moral principles, Mack would have appeared to be the perfect mentor for young Matty. And the American League – with its emphasis on clean baseball for the entire family – seemed the ideal stage.

Plus, when the Giants released their reserve list, Matty's name was not included. To his mind, he was a free agent.

"I thought I had been cast off by New York," he said. "Therefore, when Connie Mack offered me $1,200 to pitch for the Athletics, I signed with him."

Mack even sent Matty a $50 advance to buy books and supplies at Bucknell.

Not so fast . . .

"This unintentional blunder," said Matty, "got me in the worst trouble of my life."

What the collegian did not know was that Andrew Freedman, the Giants' owner, had worked a suspicious deal with Cincinnati. First, the Reds bought Matty's contract for the "joke price" of $300, then traded his rights back to the Giants for veteran pitcher Amos Rusie. The "Hoosier Thunderbolt" had been the fastest and most feared pitcher in organized ball, but now his arm was essentially dead and he hadn't pitched in two seasons. The Rusie-Mathewson deal is still considered one of the worst trades ever made – an old, washed-up flamethrower for the young, soon-to-become greatest pitcher of all time. But, there were actually two side notes of interest. First, Freedman had no intention of paying Norfolk the $2,000 he still owed for buying the rights to Mathewson the previous season and figured the maneuver would pass the debt onto the Reds. Second, and even more suspect, was that the owner of the Reds – John T. Brush – would soon become the majority owner of the Giants.

"Apparently there were considerable shenanigans afoot," said sportswriter Fred Lieb.

Of course, this was occurring in the middle of the heightened war between the two leagues. There were interleague player disputes going on in every baseball city. If Matty joined the Athletics, what could the Giants do?

The volatile Freedman was generally despised for his greed, contempt, and a host of questionable ventures. The owner was so cheap that he made the Giants hold spring training at the cold and damp Polo Grounds, also called Manhattan Stadium.

Ordering Christy to his New York office, Freedman threatened to sue the youngster if he jumped to the American League, a seditious group that he predicted would never survive.

"Freedman would blacklist me for life," Christy reported of the conversation. "He would put me out of baseball forever."

Christy caved, but confessed that he had already spent the $50 advance from the Athletics. Freedman assured Matty that he would return the money. During the season, when Christy found out that Freedman had not kept his word, he personally sent the money to the Athletics owner and manager. While Mack would soon forgive Christy, in the spring of '01, he was furious that the deal had been broken.

Whatever the drama, when Christy Mathewson left Lewisburg in March 1901 for the Giants spring training camp in New York City, he had every intention of returning to Bucknell for his senior year. For starters, he had visions of leading the Bison to an undefeated football season. Even more important, he would be back with Jenny Stoughton.

CHAPTER SIX

June 1901 . . . Polo Grounds
Matty stared out at the right field wall, his eyes wandering aimlessly to the expanse of Coogan's Bluff, scarcely paying attention to the game, much less noticing any activity in the rest of the Giants' dugout . . . which, as always, seemed locked in another universe.

Christy Mathewson's first major-league victory occurred Opening Day 1901, allowing only four hits in besting the Brooklyn Superbas 5-3. He would win his first eight games, the streak finally clipped by the Cardinals, 1-0. The turnstiles began to click, rooters anxious to see "The Boy Wonder from Bucknell." Even women and children were starting to attend games when Matty was pitching. On July 4, the Giants were actually in first place.

Mathewson would finish the season with a 20-17 record and 2.41 ERA. Okay, he heaved a miserable 23 wild pitches, worst in the National League. But he completed 36 of his 38 starts and tossed five shutouts, including a no-hitter at St. Louis, the first of the new century.

"He was the toast of New York," wrote sportswriter Fred Lieb, "as he kept the Giants, a tail-ender in 1900, in the thick of the race."

Unfortunately, the '01 Giants would eventually freefall into seventh place, 37 games behind champion Pittsburgh and only one game ahead of last-place Cincinnati, where Amos Rusie had pitched three disastrous games and retired.

According to the press, the Giants were filled with "knockers, shirkers, and loafers." Still quiet and aloof, Matty was never accepted to the inner circle of misfits, his station becoming the distant corner of the dugout . . . an outcast. Coacher George Davis and catcher Frank Bowerman tried to run interference, but the contempt only grew. The lumbering Giants had a chemistry that accepted defeat as but another day at the park, openly suspecting that the competitive college kid was trying too hard to win, purposely trying to show them up.

Some were suspicious, others downright jealous, particularly since Matty was the unparalleled favorite with the fans. Kip Selbach and Mike Grady refused to even speak to the pitcher. Piano Legs Hickman (also known as "Cheerful Charlie") told the youngster to "go back to the woods, you ain't playin' with college boys no more." To the haters, Mathewson was an aristocratic, high-nosed intellectual who undoubtedly thought he was better than them. They also didn't appreciate that the rookie had a lucrative $1,500 contract. The older players had also given him the nickname of "Sis," a poke at his somewhat tenor voice.

Although his ego and emotions routinely took a beating, Matty believed that adversity would simply make him tougher. As President Harris had said back at Bucknell, "character alone shines by its own light."

Christy continued to disregard the idiots. After all, he had a different focus.

Chicago, St. Louis, Boston, Philadelphia, Pittsburgh . . . the booming cities were glorious and the train provided a sanctuary to read. From *The Will to Believe* by William James ("do I go with my fear of being wrong, or my hope of being right?") to *Les Miserables* by Victor Hugo ("a man is not idle because he is absorbed in thought"), Christy enjoyed working his mind, opening it to all possible angles. Along with the book he was currently reading, Christy always carried – and read – the bible his parents had given to him when he left home for college.

He also devoured the newspapers, the world of 1901 in turmoil. There was the Boxer Rebellion in China and Boer War in South Africa. In defining foreign policy, vice-president Theodore Roosevelt proclaimed the United States should "speak softly and carry a big stick."

On September 6, President William McKinley was shot in Buffalo, New York. And when McKinley died the following week, Teddy Roosevelt became the nation's 26th president. Meanwhile, the worst hurricane in U.S. history killed more than 8,000 people in Galveston, Texas.

On the road, Matty enjoyed the upscale restaurants and lavish 25-cent dinners, but almost always dined alone. He certainly didn't spend his money in a barroom partying with his dimwitted teammates. To Matty, life was to be enjoyed strictly on his own terms, within his own principles . . . no matter the mentality of the pack. Plus, he was stubborn. They mocked him, so he ignored them.

Toward the end of the season, several of Christy's teammates suggested he ask the team owner for a raise.

Freedman – who had threatened Matty with a lawsuit six months earlier – had little interest in baseball other than the lucrative profit margin from playing in the nation's largest city. An arrogant and ruthless business tycoon with an explosive temper, Freedman preferred his fleet of yachts and nights at the opera. Other than his corrupt political cronies at Tammany Hall, no one seemed to like him.

Still, Christy's teammates insisted that he deserved more money. Of course, he wasn't fooled by their sudden, heartfelt interest in his financial worth . . . he knew they were setting him up. In fact, Freedman once fined Amos Rusie $200 for the audacity to ask for a raise.

Funny thing was that Freedman actually liked Matty. As for more money, he instead offered him two new suits, which the young hurler badly needed. The deal gave his teammates a few extra chuckles, but Christy was looking sharp. And he was even more pleased several weeks later when Freedman offered him a new contract for the next season at a salary of $3,000 with a $500 signing bonus. At a time when the average worker earned just over 20 cents an hour, Matty would be making more than twice that amount per pitch.

After a long and deep evaluation of his future, Christy decided not to return for his senior year at Bucknell, figuring he could finish his education after baseball. Still, he might as well have gone back to college, considering the amount of time he spent in Lewisburg visiting

Jane. There no longer seemed any reason to mask their intentions, although her father was furious that Christy had dropped out of school.

Christy gallantly attempted to explain his reasoning to Frank Stoughton. Yes, he would like to earn a degree, but because he was now receiving such a lucrative salary, he needed to concentrate entirely on baseball, spending the offseason thinking about strengths and weaknesses of the players he had pitched against. While not a common practice, it seemed reasonable to Christy that he prepare his energetic mind to capture every possible advantage. Since Jane's father still did not consider baseball a productive occupation, Frank most likely was not convinced . . . even though he was slowly becoming fond of the man his daughter so deeply loved.

Certainly, it had not been an easy decision for Matty. Always blessed with an intellectual drive, he loved Bucknell and the college life. However, now 21, he was no longer preparing for a career, he had found it . . . and was both stubborn and smart enough to realize the importance of mastering his profession.

The Bucknell football team would need to find a new fullback and kicker in 1901, Doc Hoskins' club notching a 6-4 record. Harvard and Michigan both finished undefeated, opening a national argument as to which school should be national champion.

Out in California, the Tournament of Roses Parade had been an annual event since 1890 and included such supplementary activities as tug-of-war, bronco busting, and ostrich races. But on New Years Day 1902, the parade planners had decided to add a football game to the agenda with Stanford (3-1-2) representing the west and Michigan (10-0) the east. The Wolverines arrived in Pasadena with the impressive statistic of having outscored their opponents 501-0 (poor Buffalo had been pounded 128-0).

Played on the campus of Cal Tech, the first Rose Bowl – known then as the "Tournament East-West Football Game" – proved brutally lopsided. After three quarters, with mighty Michigan hammering his team 49-0, the Stanford captain conceded the game. The following year, the parade organizers replaced football with a polo match. It would be 14 years before the Rose Bowl became the official addition to the parade.

No doubt Christy missed the hard knocks and glory of college football, but he had set his course, firmly believing that one of the keys to a successful baseball career was this intriguing concept of strategic pitching. He knew he had great athletic ability – throwing a baseball was easy. Why not add one of his unique strengths to the equation – outsmart the opposing hitters. With dedication and brains, Matty would turn twirling into an art.

Unfortunately, there was nothing artistic about the 1902 Giants. They did not play with their brains or their hearts, the same old complacency seemingly prevalent from opening day, the boys actually "singing and whistling merrily in the clubhouse after losing games."

Plus, there was the same despicable treatment of Mathewson. Selbach, Grady, and Hickman had moved to other teams, but the disdain for the star hurler remained.

Rookie outfielder Jack Hendricks called the treatment of Mathewson "shameless." Hendricks, who would someday manage Cincinnati, alleged that those who despised Matty "deliberately missed grounders and short-legged flies" when he was on the mound. Hendricks also insisted that Mathewson was not without fault, feeding the animosity by always keeping his distance and "acting like a pinhead." According to Hendricks, the Giants were "the rankest apology for a first-class team ever imposed upon any major-league city."

Matty finally revolted. "I cannot win with them behind me," he charged. And, of course, the hatred sweltered.

New York also had a parade of new coaches in '02, beginning with Horace Fogel and Heinie Smith. Both crumbled to the team's lethargic mentality as it slid deeper into the National League cellar. The club was so off kilter that Fogel thought it might be a good idea to also let Christy play first base. According to Hendricks, shortstop Joe Bean "delighted in sending throws into the dirt to make the college-educated first baseman look ridiculous."

While it would later become imbedded in baseball lore that Fogel somehow believed that Christy would make a better infielder than pitcher, it was hardly true.

"I managed the club for only a few weeks," said Fogel. "I had a terrible team, my first baseman was hurt and Matty was a strong, husky kid who could hit. So I put him on first when he wasn't pitching. This never was intended to be other than an emergency measure."

What Christy did not know was that behind the scenes a melodrama was developing that would soon rock the entire organization.

On July 17, 1902, Freedman hired a new manager . . . not just any manager . . . but the legendary John "Muggsy" McGraw. First, players dare not call him "Muggsy." And second, any slackers had best pack their bags. McGraw immediately released nine players, including Joe Bean, who had committed 32 errors in 50 games at short. Even light-hitting rookie Jack Hendricks got the axe.

"There is a story that McGraw fired me off the team the moment he saw me swing," Hendricks would tell sportswriter Frank Graham. "Fired me off the Giants the first day. That is a lie. I hid in the clubhouse the first day. McGraw never fired me until the second day."

Also known as "Little Napoleon" for his strategic guile, McGraw was 29 years old when he came to New York, leaving Baltimore the same way he had arrived . . . in a firestorm. Only in his third year of managing, he was still a superb infielder and batsman. In an age of brutes, Muggsy McGraw was widely considered the game's most ferocious and twisted competitor, the *Baltimore Herald* calling him "a whole team and a dog under the wagon."

John "Little Napoleon" McGraw.

McGraw was rude and violent, a brawler and bully. From blistering threats and tantrums, he redefined vulgarity with a fiery temper that often fueled streaks of near insanity. At a time when ballgames carried only one umpire, the cagey third baseman secretly grabbed or outright tripped opposing base runners. Observed one umpire, "McGraw eats gunpowder every morning and washes it down with warm blood."

With contempt as his flag, McGraw loved confrontation. On the road, Manager McGraw would purposely have his Giants put on their uniforms at the hotel, then ride in horseback carriages through the opposing city on their way to the ballpark. The players snickered as hostile fans threw tomatoes in Pittsburgh, rocks in Philly. Armed for battle, the Giants always fired back. It was good for ticket sales, beamed McGraw. Little Napoleon was viewed as a "venomous viper" everywhere but New York, where he was loved for his spunk, his theater, and his refusal to lose.

Said Blanche McGraw of her husband, "When he and his team took the field, everyone on the other side, including the batboy, was his mortal enemy."

If he didn't like a judgment, he was known to pull his team from the field and once even locked out an umpire from getting into the ballpark the following day. That he had actually managed the Baltimore Orioles might seem puzzling, since the American League was founded as an alternative to the wicked lunacy of the National League. But, because the AL owners wanted Baltimore in the fold, the immensely popular McGraw had been hired. While Muggsy agreed to reform his rowdy ways, his definition of good behavior proved significantly flexible. Of course, what followed was a long list of fines, suspensions, and final warnings.

As the two leagues battled for superiority, there was often more commotion in the backrooms than the field. Riding an indefinite suspension from AL president Ban Johnson, McGraw leveraged $7,000 that he was owed by the Orioles to win his release and then signed a lucrative $11,000 contract with the Giants, making him the highest paid man baseball, player or coach. With new majority owner John T. Brush giving him complete control to rebuild the club, McGraw immediately lured four strong players and the groundskeeper from the Orioles.

Little Napoleon was a natural for the rough-and-tumble National League, perfect for New York City. His players called him Mr. McGraw and, quite frankly, most adored the man. He was tough, demanding those under his command to always give their best and battle to the bitter end. But he also was protective of those who followed his command, at times like a father to a child.

"Any mental error, any failure to think, and McGraw would be all over you," said outfielder Fred Snodgrass. "And I do believe he had the most vicious tongue of any man who ever lived. Sometimes that wasn't very easy to take, you know. However, he'd never get on you for a mechanical mistake, a fielding error, or failure to get a hit."

McGraw designed his Giants to be mean, scrappy, and vocal. While able to match their boss in exuberance, they understood that McGraw would always lead the charge, the fiery Little Napoleon dishing the venom and cursing the consequences.

Said Grantland Rice: "His very walk across the field in a hostile town is a challenge to the multitudes."

In 16 seasons as a player, McGraw would notch a .344 career batting average. In 30 years managing the Giants, he would claim 10 pennants and three world championships. He would be elected to the Hall of Fame in 1937, one year after the inaugural class that included Matty.

John McGraw and Christy Mathewson . . . forever linked within the lore of baseball . . . and yet so totally different . . . as if coexistence would be impossible . . .

It would make a wonderful clash for the dime novels – Matty the clean and polite country boy versus Muggsy the rude and brawling city kid. They were polar opposites in size, looks, character, and noise level. Christy had the idyllic childhood and Johnny McGraw ran away from an abusive father. Matty was Protestant, Muggsy Irish Catholic. Matty was the All-American hero and Little Napoleon the villainous egomaniac. The list of disparities seemed endless.

Which might explain why the *New York Tribune* reported when the new boss arrived in July 1902 that Mathewson would be shipped to St. Louis "as it is believed that he and McGraw are not on the best of terms." That presumption was wrong. McGraw loved Matty's potential, adding that it was "sheer insanity" to have even experimented with the young pitcher as a first sacker.

"The finest pitching motion I ever saw," said McGraw. "He'll pitch from now on."

Of course, McGraw could not have possibly realized the soon-to-unfold scope of the youngster's success . . . or, for that matter, his own role in Matty's vault to the top of the universe.

For starters, there was work to be done.

"By constant efforts at speed, he had become wild," said McGraw. "He simply knew nothing about pitching at all. His wonderful equipment was being wasted."

One other important piece of business was that McGraw immediately established a new clubhouse environment, making it quite clear that the days of hassling or bullying the club's young ace had ended. In fact, friendship throughout the team was now a requirement, lest the perpetrator care to test the wrath of McGraw. Of course, Little Napoleon had already fired most of Matty's old tormenters.

When the 1902 season ended, the Giants were dead last at 48-88, Pittsburgh lapping the field at 103-36. McGraw, however, was not worried. He had brought four of his favorites from Baltimore – Roger Bresnahan, Jack Cronin, Dan McGann, and Joe "Iron Man" McGinnity – and was intent on adding even more firepower to the roster he had retained. In fact, the new manager had spent much of the last two months of the season away from the team, scouting for potential replacements. McGraw figured that Mathewson, McGinnity, and Luther "Dummy" Taylor – with a quality team behind them – could dominate.

While encouraged that McGraw had his back, Matty was disturbed that he had finished with a 14-17 record, even if it was a lousy team. Sure, he had led the league with eight shutouts and registered a sharp 2.12 ERA. *The Sporting News* marveled that Mathewson "is regarded throughout the country as the game's greatest pitcher."

Christy appreciated the thought, but he had to wonder if perhaps the Giants would forever be a second-rate team . . . that McGraw was just blowing smoke.

"Matty knows there's only one New York in the land," editorialized the *St. Louis Post-Dispatch*, "but to linger with a tail-ender is hardly palatable to any first-class player."

The St. Louis Browns, on the other hand, were a team with great promise, having finished second in the American League behind Connie Mack's Athletics. The owner of the Browns, Robert Hedges, had made a fortune producing carriages, but wisely changed course when he surmised that automobiles would own the future. Friendly and honest,

Hedges had created a family environment at Sportsman Park by refusing to sell alcohol and hiring security guards to ensure the peace.

Toward the end of the '02 season, with the Giants stuck in last and their new manager, McGraw, scouring the country for talent, Hedges asked Matty to consider pitching for the Browns in '03. Matty had always liked St. Louis, the nation's fourth largest city. And his salary would be doubled. Matty agreed, excited to be heading west.

Okay, he had signed two contracts, but jumpers and double-jumpers were everywhere, the AL-NL "salary wars" having created a golden bonanza for ballplayers.

"It will not be long before every star player in the country will carry a lawyer around with him," lamented *Sporting Life*. "This business of a player changing his mind every day, a sort of 'contracts fresh every hour' is growing very ridiculous."

So don't be surprised that Matty decided to sign a third contract . . . to play professional football. The Polo Grounds had barely closed its gates on the '02 season when he headed west to play fullback and kicker for the Pittsburgh Stars of the brand new National Football League (no relation to the current NFL). The Saturday league only had three teams, the two Philadelphia elevens (Athletics and Phillies) run by the baseball franchises. Playing in the North Shore Coliseum, the Stars recorded a 3-2-1 mark before claiming the "World Championship" with an 11-0 victory over the Athletics. Lacking organization and money, the first NFL would fold after one season.

For Matty, football could not end fast enough, cutting his season short and returning to Central Pennsylvania to ask Jane for her hand in marriage.

Three of the parents were thrilled. Jane's father was still not convinced. And regarding the state of Matty's two contracts, no telling what Frank Stoughton thought.

If anyone understood the art of jumping teams, it was McGraw, who immediately tracked down his wayward hurler and asked him to double-jump back to the Giants. But Christy had been burned before and, to his stubbornly calculated thinking, it was all business.

"I like New York, but McGraw has got to show me that he is going to have a winning aggregation, and then offer me a fat contract if he wants to sign me," said Matty. "I would be foolish if I didn't get all the money I can. A pitcher's professional career is short at the best, and it behooves him to look out for himself."

The obvious factor in the battle for major-league supremacy was that the American League was winning. Trumpeting its clean brand of baseball, the AL had not only stolen many of the NL's stars, but also outdrew the older circuit at the gate by 31 percent in 1902. Every day seemed to bring a new controversy and heightened accusations.

"Reports of dealings and double dealings, leads and counters, cross and double cross," wrote the *St. Louis Post-Dispatch*. "It is a merry war of rumors . . . ricocheting through the baseball world."

Finally, the two leagues reached an agreement, if for nothing else than to blunt the massive pay scales. *The Sporting News* reported that the compromise was essentially "horse-trading" – some players were sent back to their original teams, some stayed. But the underlying carrot was that a new American League franchise would be placed in New York City. Not wanting a new neighbor, John T. Brush vehemently opposed the move, but found no sympathy from any other owner. It was decided that the old Baltimore club would become the New York Highlanders (the original Yankees). While Brush fumed, Robert Hedges made a peace offering by giving Mathewson's contract back to the Giants.

"My individual and club interests were of comparatively minor importance when the future of baseball was at stake," said the owner of the Browns. "Somebody had to make concessions."

Including Brush, who gave Matty a new $4,000 contract with a $1,000 bonus.

Closer to home, it was Frank Stoughton making the concessions. Grudgingly at first, the old railroad supervisor finally gave his blessing to the marriage of Jane and Christy . . . never once to be disappointed.

"We did not intend to get married until we felt we could afford it," said Jane. "We knew that living in New York was going to be higher, but with such an income we thought we could risk it."

The Lewisburg newspaper, which could be delivered to a customer's doorstep for a dollar per year (in advance), carried the wedding announcement that included the observation that it was not until Christy had left Bucknell that "the town busybodies regarded his intentions as serious."

On March 5, 1903, Christy and Jane were married at the Stoughton home on Market Street. Rev. Wellington Thomas of the First Presbyterian Church conducted the ceremony before 150 guests. Jane's youngest sister, Margaret, was the Maid of Honor and Christy's Bucknell roommate and fraternity brother, Ernest Sterling, was the Best Man. Louise Albright, who had introduced the couple, also had a role in the wedding party.

The newspaper proclaimed it "one of the most fashionable weddings of the season" and noted that the new Mrs. Mathewson was "a lady of charming disposition and an energetic church worker."

Although raised a Baptist, Christy agreed to a pre-marriage trade with Jane . . . he became a Presbyterian and she a Republican.

The couple would honeymoon in Savannah, Georgia, a romantic destination that was also the site of the Giants spring training camp, the new owner putting an end to March baseball in New York.

At the train station located across the Susquehanna River in Milton, the newlyweds boarded the Buffalo Flyer to Washington D.C. It would have been nice to have a clean getaway, but Christy's Phi Gamma Delta fraternity brothers had other ideas, passing out flyers to the boarding passengers that read, "Christy Mathewson, New York's great baseball pitcher, and newly wedded wife are on this train. Make them feel at home as there may be 'something doing.' Note: He will be easily recognized by his boyish countenance and Apollo-like form."

CHAPTER SEVEN

Spring Training 1903 . . . Savannah, Georgia

Jane Stoughton Mathewson knew that the woman in the fancy dress must be the manager's wife. Adding to Jane's discomfort, there were few places to hide in the lobby of the DeSoto Hotel.

Blanche McGraw didn't look that old, but she was definitely big-city stylish . . . the sequined dress, the make-up, and that gigantic ring on her finger. Jane quickly looked away, suddenly realizing that Blanche was just as busy watching her.

"That has to be the Mathewson girl," thought Mrs. McGraw, sizing up the young bride's beauty and simple white dress . . . an image that fit perfectly into Blanche's well-thought perception of a straight-laced Sunday School teacher from Central Pennsylvania. "She probably thinks I'm a hussy," winced Blanche.

"Talk about high society," figured Jane as she stared again at the magnitude of the dazzling ring on Blanche's left finger, obviously a gift from John McGraw. Jane had heard all about him, too. "What kind of woman would be married to a man like that?"

They were both wrong. After what seemed like hours awkwardly eyeing one another, the two women – the only wives at the Giants' camp – finally reached the nerve to talk. They hit it off instantly . . . soon walking past the Live Oaks and Spanish Moss of Savannah, shopping and talking, laughing about their silly suspicions and judgments. The women became inseparable, the first days of a friendship that would last more than half a century.

"She and I just seemed to be drawn towards each other," said Jane.

"While the men were practicing," Blanche would later write, "we would stroll down Bull Street to Forsyth Park where the early spring azaleas were budding and all of life seemed green and new and full of hope."

Blanche Sindall had been born to Baltimore wealth in 1882, making her younger than both Jane and Christy. She met John McGraw – nine years her senior – while attending Mount Saint Agnes College.

After telling her husband about Jane, Blanche asked what he thought of Christy.

"I knew he was big and bulky, blond, and with big blue eyes," recalled Blanche. "John replied, 'Looks like he can pitch with his head as well as his arm,' and he honestly believed that answered my question."

When the team headed north for the new season, the McGraws asked the Mathewsons to share a home. The two couples moved into a seven-room furnished apartment at West 85th Street and Columbus Avenue, just a block from Central Park. The McGraws paid the $50 rent and the Mathewsons bought the food.

It is important to note that John McGraw at home was the antithesis of the ruthless coacher he played every afternoon.

"He was always kind, considerate, and affectionate," said Blanche.

The *Literary Digest* commented, "It doesn't seem possible that the mild mannered, gentlemanly, quiet man who shakes your hand is John McGraw."

Certainly, the early development of the friendship between Matty and his manager must have been interesting . . . like slow-dancing in the moonlight with a werewolf, careful not to step on any toes, both sizing up the other until realizing, probably like a bolt from the heavens, that their opposite personalities were somehow a perfect fit. Forget establishing any ground rules, they truly liked one another . . . a closeness that would forever be blind to their obvious differences.

Both admired the other's talents and intellect. Both respected the other's turf, accepting long-cemented personality traits with an understanding usually reserved for the closest of families. Muggsy became both best friend and father, Matty both pupil and son. Muggsy could puff out his chest and rage into battle, Matty quietly content to stay outside the fracas.

"It is the prospect of a good fight," Little Napoleon would proclaim, "that brings out the crowds."

"I have seen McGraw go onto ballfields where he is as welcome as the Black Plague," said Mathewson. "He doesn't know what fear is."

But what really made the alliance work was that both were extremely intelligent and zealous competitors, obsessed with winning baseball games, an absolute hatred for losing. Of course, Christy was a bit more philosophical at masking defeat, but it could tear him apart.

"You must have an alibi to show why you lost," he said. "If you haven't one, make one up. Your self-confidence must be maintained."

McGraw was more direct.

"The game is only fun for me when I'm winning," he said.

No matter the outcome, both were ready for another nine innings. It was always about the challenge, the game.

Life in New York City could be a challenge for Jane. She was 23 years old and had never seen a building with more than two stories. Christy had experienced the big city shock several years before when he first arrived in the majors.

Welcome to a wonderland unlike any place on earth.

The New York skyline was powerful, gigantic, and strangely stunning. Henry James described the skyscrapers as "extravagant pins in a cushion already overplanted." It was called a "limitless silhouette, a marvelous spectacle, a massive beauty."

Not everyone loved the skyline, Maxim Gorky, a writer from Russia, saying the city resembled "a huge jaw with black, uneven teeth."

New York City was prosperous – an economy based on commerce, industry, and finance. In the early 1900s, it was shipping one-third of the nation's exports and greeting two-thirds of its imports. Huge banks and insurance companies lavishly gathered assets, an "overflowing wealth" plunging into New York "as water downhill." In 1906, British author H.G. Wells called the city a "great torrent of spending and glittering prosperity."

The city was modern – a "thousand and one mechanical conveniences." When the subway opened in 1904, German dramatist Ludvig Fulda called the transportation system "a symbol of the titanic strength and energy of Americanism." Even the streets were paved. In 1908, *Harpers Monthly* quipped, "the motorist whirs through the intersecting streets and round the corners, bent on suicide or homicide."

It was electric – the lights of Broadway like "fabulous glow worms crawling up and down." Whether the pursuit was cultural or intellectual, New York was loaded. Music, theater, clubs, and cinema palaces provided nonstop entertainment. Libraries, bookstores, art galleries, and colleges invigorated the mind.

And graceful – blessed with impeccable fashion, the upper echelons of society could stroll past the grand architectural monuments to civilization, dine at elegant restaurants, and taxi through Central Park in a fine horse carriage.

New York was passionate – where soldiers gallantly marched off to World War I, then paraded again to a roaring embrace upon their glorious return.

It was gigantic – rapidly passing the capitals of the Old World to become the largest city on the planet by 1910. Seeking a better life, immigrants mostly arrived from Russia, Italy, Ireland, and Germany. In the century's first decade, more than nine million immigrants would be processed at Ellis Island.

And it was energetic – a constant stream of people, ideas, and change.

No, it was crazy – the constant clatter, the chronic construction, the urgent rush. "Noise and human hurry," lamented H.G. Wells, "the blindly furious energy of growth that must go on."

And it went much deeper. There was racism and prejudice, poverty and congestion. Women and children were packed into sweatshops and factories "like herrings in a barrel." In the dark and stuffy confines of

Frederick B. Gordon's mill, children worked 60 hours a week for three dollars. Gordon called it "charity."

While working conditions for the poor were horrendous, living in slums "thick with dirt and vermin" could be worse.

"Individuals count for nothing," wrote Wells.

Likewise, the promise for a better life died early for many immigrants, settling into the nearest ghetto for safety – drawn by the heritage, language, and culture of the world they had so desperately left behind.

And that was just a taste of the times. New York was good, bad, and all things in between.

Enter baseball, the American sport that could be shared by all. Didn't matter if you were Russian or Polish, prayed in a church or synagogue, dropped out in the second grade or had a degree from Princeton . . . the only requirement was that you could hit, catch, and throw a ball. If not, you could be a paying customer – rich people ushered to the box seats, poorer folks to the bleachers. Everyone could participate . . . unless, of course, your skin was any shade of black. If so, you had to go somewhere else to play.

It was also a time in baseball that would be known as the "Deadball Era" (1901-19), producing a spectacle of speed and strategy far different from the game that has evolved over the decades.

The spitball was not included in Matty's arsenal of pitches, but it was perfectly legal. In fact, any method of scuffing was acceptable. Balls were cut and scratched, shaved with an emery board, rubbed with talcum powder, even arrived at the plate dripping with tobacco juice. Even the "coffee ball" was fashionable, the twirler chewing coffee beans and spitting the sap between the seams of the ball. After nine innings, catchers could be a mess.

Plus, it was tradition in the early 1900s to only use one baseball per game. When a fan attempted one day to keep a foul ball, John McGraw leaped into the stands and chased him down. Every baseball took a beating. By the third inning, it was no longer white. By the sixth, the ball often resembled a clump of mush. By the ninth – as the dark shadows of late afternoon blanketed the stadium – the old onion was difficult to see, hard to hit, and brutal to field.

Another tradition that had remained intact was the acceptance of fans standing on the playing field when the bleachers became too crowded. The overflow crowd stood with their backs to the outfield wall, a rope separating them from the action. Base hits that went into the crowd, but not over the wall, were ruled triples.

It was routine at the start of the century to employ only one umpire per game, a sure ticket to chaos. While some games were assigned two officials as early as 1903, the practice became mandatory nine years later . . . yes, that controlled the rowdies.

As for political correctness, that concept was still far into the future. Note a matter-of-fact account from the *New York Times* after the Giants faced Chief Bender of the Philadelphia Athletics:

> "Back to the tepee for you," hooted a rooter.
>
> "Giants grab heap much wampum," yelled another, giving an imitation Indian yell.
>
> "Let's fix the Indian," yelled John McGraw from the coachers box.
>
> "I'm sorry, old Pitch-Em-Heap, but here's where you go back to the reservation," New York's Mike Donlin remarked while stepping to the plate.
>
> Apparently, Chief Bender had heard it all before. "Your conclusion, Mr. Donlin, is right in this immediate vicinity," answered Bender as Donlin cut off three slices of air and walked away a heart-broken man.

It should be mentioned that Bender, a member of Minnesota's Ojibwa tribe and future Hall of Famer, had attended Dickinson College and, like Mathewson, was considered one of the most intelligent pitchers in the game. Also, like Matty, he was extremely kind and considerate. He was a painter, entrepreneur, and world-class trap shooter. But, it was an age of ingrained stereotypes.

Of course, McGraw was hassled for being Irish Catholic, Luther "Dummy" Taylor for being deaf, and Mordecai Brown for missing two fingers. At the time, the circle of slurs was considered an integral part of baseball custom.

Early in his career, Mathewson was routinely blistered for his educational background, but passed the test by becoming stronger with each new insult.

"Lay off the Mathewson kid," Brooklyn manager Ned Hanlon finally ordered. "He likes the chatter you fellows are spilling."

Oh, there was plenty of jabbering between coaches and players. Even Cy Young tried to badger Ty Cobb with reference to his southern heritage.

"Too bad Sherman didn't do more to Georgia when he was down your way," Young shouted from the mound. "He left too many corncobs lying around."

"I'm going to drive the next one down your throat," Cobb yelled back, "and they can cart you off to the cemetery."

There were few homeruns during the Deadball Era, the National League registering only 101 for the entire 1907 season. Even the introduction of cork-center balls around 1911 didn't immediately dent the fences. Frank "Home Run" Baker of the Athletics earned his nickname for hitting TWO out of the park in the 1911 World Series. Baker led the American League for four straight seasons, a personal-high of 12 homers in 1913. The big slugger, however, was Gavvy Cravath of the Philadelphia Phillies. A California boy from the avocado groves of Escondido, Cactus Gavvy led the National League six times, his record 24 homers in 1915 ultimately cracked four years later when Babe Ruth belted 29.

It might have been that the players were stronger, equipment more modern, or spitballs were finally declared illegal. Whatever, when Ruth followed with seasons of 54 and 59 homers, the "Deadball Era" was officially over.

With the beginning of the 1903 season, the relationship between the Mathewsons and McGraws was already quite comfortable. The women cooked the meals and often played cards while the men talked baseball. When the men could be pulled from their work, the four best friends settled in for a relaxing game of bridge.

McGraw was an infielder, but did appreciate the skill and science of throwing, always willing to discuss ideas. Theirs was a journey of strategy and discovery, two artists working their passion, kindred spirits from opposite sides of everything but baseball. And the admiration was genuinely sincere, neither questioning nor attempting to manipulate the other's character or beliefs . . . poster boys for harmony.

They could chatter late into the night, both maintaining a mental sharpness that often pushed past the border of genius. To them, the subject and dialogue was riveting.

The Giants' coacher found that the youngster possessed a hunger to learn with an intelligence ranging far above the average ballplayer.

"I never had to tell Mathewson anything a second time. From that first day, it seemed, Matty carefully studied all opposing batters. Once he learned what they could hit and what they couldn't, he never forgot."

"Anytime someone got a hit off me, I made a mental note of the pitch," said Matty. "He'd never see that one again."

Mathewson, of course, possessed a busy and brilliant mind that enjoyed most any topic.

"He had an unusual mind, a quick mind, and the stubbornness of a person with a trained mind," recalled Blanche. "He had the ego of a great competitor and a deep-rooted belief that every opponent was his inferior."

Add to that the windfall of a photographic memory.

"When he played checkers, his response to a move was drawn from his memory of the proper defense," said Blanche. "It wasn't even necessary for him to see the board at checkers or chess, which enabled him to defeat eight or ten really good players while blindfolded . . . and he would talk about the most common opening, Old 14th, or its countless variations as long as you would listen."

Little Napoleon also had a fabulous memory, but only concerning baseball. As a player, he had carefully studied the strengths and weaknesses of every pitcher. He knew habits and quirks, the ability to recall every pitch of a ballgame. And absolutely no one better understood the tactics of the game.

"They were happy in their scheming, because the Giants were a winning team," said Blanche. "We couldn't realize, of course, that they were making baseball history by sheer force of personality and determination. Nothing else, in my opinion, can account for the Polo Grounds miracle of 1903 and 1904."

With McGraw as mentor, Mathewson was now studying every hitter. Outfielder Roger Bresnahan, who would be moved to catcher in 1905, continually traded strategic notes with the young pitcher. It was non-stop learning as Matty practiced his fadeaway, perfected his control, and picked up a devastating change-up from Joe "Iron Man" McGinnity.

Now there was a teacher. Nobody on the club was tougher than Iron Man. The future Hall of Famer had been a miner, a muleskinner, and worked in a foundry. At one time he owned a saloon, employing himself as the only bouncer. Twenty-eight years old when he hit the majors, Iron Man had a vicious side-armed curve he called "Old Sal" and a seemingly indestructible arm. In 1903, he pitched both ends of three doubleheaders in one month, winning all six games.

Matty, Muggsy, and Iron Man.

"It was difficult for a batter to get McGinnity's measure," said Connie Mack. "Sometimes his fingers would almost scrape the ground as he hurled the ball. He knew all the tricks for putting a batter on the spot."

Matty and Iron Man were the best one-two punch in baseball for seven seasons, one or the other always leading the league in victories.

In an era when a good starting pitcher might throw 400 innings a season and seldom be relieved, Matty learned how to pace his strength. Perhaps never in the game before or since has there been a pitcher who could give up so many hits in the early and middle innings to eventual runners who would never score. If the Giants had a hefty lead, he purposely cruised. In the late innings, he took no prisoners.

"He seldom wasted energy early in a game," said McGraw. "In a pinch, when a hit meant a run or the game, he was as close to invincible as any pitcher could get."

Mathewson, a rapid worker, once threw a 14-hit shutout, allowing singles to the first two batters of each inning until the eighth. He retired the final six hitters in order.

Another time, an early six-run advantage that had been whittled to 6-5 by the ninth inning.

"Bear down, you big baboon," McGraw yelled from the dugout.

"Take it easy, Mac, it's more fun this way," replied Matty, who then struck out the final three batters.

Matty got the start for the 1903 Opening Day at the Polo Grounds, but got hammered by Brooklyn, 9-7. Four days later, at Brooklyn's Washington Park, he tamed the Superbas, 2-1, with a three-hitter. He was just warming up. On May 16, a crowd of 31,500 poured into the Polo Grounds to see Christy Mathewson – New York City's first baseball star – lead the first-place Giants past the defending champion' Pirates. McGraw was in jovial mood. Over in the American League, the crosstown Highlanders were floundering in sixth place.

Although the Giants seemed to always lead the league in attendance (they drew 302,875 fans for a last-place team in 1902), the new product doubled the draw. In 1903, McGraw's first full season as manager, attendance skied to 579,530 and would soar the following season to 609,826 fans. As majority owner, John T. Brush commenced a liberal pay scale for his employees. After all, the personable Brush was making a fortune, especially when Mathewson was pitching.

The expansive Polo Grounds offered a fine afternoon away from the exuberant pace of the city in '03. The new subway was still being constructed, so the best way to reach the wooden stadium was by elevated train. Rooters also came by horse-drawn carriages or an excursion boat up the Harlem River. Box seats cost $1.25 with general admission at 75 cents. The first 100 fans could get into the bleachers for a quarter each, then 40 cents after that. Stretching across right field, the cranks on Coogan's Bluff watched for free.

More and more, Matty was the rage of Gotham.

"He won every heart in town," recalled Blanche McGraw, who also might have carried a secret crush. "He was nearly six feet two inches with two hundred pounds of well-conditioned body. He read a lot."

He had also become a favorite in the dugout. McGraw was indeed the master manipulator. His creation of the happy Giants' family was part by command and understanding, part because he proclaimed himself as the only person his players were allowed to despise. At Little Napoleon's command, the ridicule toward Matty quickly eased, the tension dissipated. It helped that the pitcher had showed a wealth of maturity by lightening up and dropping the condescending facade. To the new and mature Matty, it didn't matter that half the team had never finished elementary school or no longer attended church. He communicated, showed respect, listened, and joked. Okay, he was different, but his teammates soon discovered that he was amazingly interesting. He opened to them, they opened to him . . . and suddenly he was one of the boys. Now respected for his talent and brains, Matty greatly enjoyed the newfound stature.

"Matty never thought he was better than anybody else," said teammate Rube Marquard. "It was just the way he carried himself. But it was okay, because when you came to it, Matty *was* different."

If McGraw ever instructed Matty on the talent of making friends, it is unlikely. It was certainly a bonus that Mathewson was amiable to the newly established team camaraderie. But the bottom line was that

McGraw had made it possible for Matty to be himself. It was long overdue, but what a relief.

With a keen sense of public relations, McGraw understood how to interest and sway reporters, spicing his volatile passion for the game with a seemingly endless stream of great quotes.

"I am absolute czar," he boasted. "My men know it. I order plays and they obey. If they don't, I fine them."

Little Napoleon and his Giants were suddenly big news. And, within the belly of the monster, stood Matty . . . the college education, the untarnished image, the fertile mind, the uncharted talent. It was truly ironic that baseball's master of insurgency was Christy Mathewson's first and only press agent.

But, while McGraw was a sportswriter's dream, Matty could be reserved.

"He disliked having people – even teammates – close in on him," said Fred Lieb.

"A cold and distant personality until you knew him well," wrote Damon Runyon of Matty. "No hand shaker. No seeker of the limelight of publicity. But he had a character that would have made him great in any calling."

And while Muggsy would be one to happily slap a sportswriter on the back, throw out a few wonderful quotes and go about his way, Christy was much more cerebral, steady . . . more interested in the writer's life than the questions.

"Matty was not given to loose talk and it was that characteristic that gave some the impression that he was cold," said Bozeman Bulger. "As a matter of fact his sympathy was intense. He looked on life just as he did on pitching . . . the details had to be just so."

It all mixed together with a perfect blend of timing. Remember, professional baseball players were still generally viewed as a bunch of uneducated thugs bashing each other over the head on a warm summer afternoon. A transfusion of purity was precisely what the industry most needed – a new look of decency, respectability.

And so the legend of the Boy Wonder began to percolate. Here was a college kid who embraced sportsmanship and moral strength, a new breed of ballplayer, the Christian Gentleman . . . and coached by Muggsy McGraw, of all people.

Stories spread in newspapers and magazines from the big cities to the farmlands. Who was this tall, good-looking kid with grit and brains and manners?

Of course, had Matty been anything below brilliant, all the hype in the world could not have carved him into this brand new baseball god of all things pure and wonderful.

Just ask the Pirates. The defending champs had outdistanced New York by 53.5 games the previous season, but those days had vanished. In early June of '03, the Giants had a six-game lead, Matty having already beaten Honus Wagner and crew four times. A Pittsburgh sportswriter observed that when Matty was scheduled to pitch, the Pirates were "apparently beaten before they put on their uniforms."

After Matty cruised to a 10-2 victory to open a three-game series at Exposition Park, The Flying Dutchman had seen enough.

"Spit on your bat and hit the ball," Wagner commanded his team-mates before the second game. They did, notching consecutive shutouts and jumping back into the hunt.

The turnaround was so frustrating for the Giants that even Matty lost his composure. Arguing a call while coaching third base, he was ejected for kicking dirt at umpire James Johnston. The outburst most likely surprised everyone, particularly Jimmy Sebring and Bucky Veil. The two Pirate rookies had been freshmen at Bucknell when Matty was a superstar upperclassman, so pardon their shock at seeing a hero getting tossed.

Eventually, the Pirates would capture their third straight NL crown, but don't blame Mathewson, who went 8-0 against the champs and 30-13 overall as the Giants stormed from the cellar to second.

Jimmy Sebring of the Pirates was the perfect ballplayer. The 6-foot, 180-pound outfielder from Bucknell was strong, talented, and fast . . . a natural hitter with a rifle arm . . . and the striking looks of a matinee idol.

The early years of what surely would be a splendid career featured a slew of game-winning dramatics, rave reviews from the baseball elite, and a love affair with the Pittsburgh fans. "Jeems" would even hit the first home run in World Series history, against Cy Young in Game One at Boston. Although the Pirates would lose the 1903 Series, Sebring topped everyone with a .367 batting average.

The Sporting Life projected that the youngster just might be better than Honus Wagner.

But a string of illnesses and injuries pushed his return home to Williamsport, Pennsylvania, where he starred for the local baseball team. Plagued by a bad leg, his attempts to get back to the majors continually bombed. In late December of 1909, Jimmy Sebring suffered a seizure and died. He was only 27 years old.

In 1904, Harry Stevens invented a career at the Polo Grounds. Wearing a dazzling red coat and matching top hat, Stevens wandered the stands selling nickel scorecards and roasted peanuts. Armed with a thunderous voice, the good-natured Stevens supported a wife and five children with his earnings.

Well, cheering for the Giants not only was fashionable, it was a passion.

McGraw's construction of a powerhouse was swift, the Giants winning it all in 1904, their 106-47 record besting the runner-up Cubs by 13 games. Matty *improved* to 33-12 with a 2.03 ERA and a team-leading 212 strikeouts, but he was not the ace of the staff. Iron Man McGinnity, a decade older than Christy, had a career-best 35-8 mark with a 1.61 ERA. Matty and McGinnity might well have won more games had there been a postseason. Winners of the first World Series, Boston had repeated as champions of the American League. Led by veteran pitcher Cy Young and superstar outfielder Tris Speaker, the Americans were primed for a showdown with the Giants.

Slow down . . .

Since there were no definite arrangements that a series had to be played, John T. Brush argued that his players didn't need to prove themselves against an inferior product. McGraw seconded the opinion, claiming that the New York Giants were the champs of the "only real major league."

Brush, who at times did not know when to stop talking, then called Boston "a minor league town."

Brush might as well have dumped gasoline on fire. Even the *New York World* called the slur against the City of Boston "so stupid it will not even deceive the bat boys at the Polo Grounds."

What angered the baseball public even more was the avoidance of a championship series. *The Sporting News* called the Giants "disgraceful," adding that Brush was "so internally selfish that it chills the blood of every true sportsman."

That said, the owners of both leagues quickly agreed upon rules for a World Series beginning the next season, 1905. Young would be 38 years old by then and still six years from retirement, but his team was beginning to tumble. And McGraw, with his ace not yet 25, had a juggernaut. Of course, anyone who had not heard of Christy Mathewson by '05 was simply not paying attention . . . for the legend was beginning to take a life of its own.

CHAPTER EIGHT

August 1905 . . . Nickel Plate Road

Christy was lost in a book; his focus riveted on Jack London's The Call of the Wild . . . life in the Alaskan wilderness and the mighty sled dog, Buck . . .

> "And when, on the still cold nights, he pointed his nose at a star and howled long and wolflike, it was his ancestors, dead and dust, pointing nose at star and howling down through the centuries and through him."

Somewhere in the far reaches of his mind, Christy factored that it still must be at least several hundred miles to Chicago, but the thought was fleeting . . . despite the rumbling bumps and sways, he had forgotten that he was riding the train, the NKP (New York, Chicago, and St. Louis Railway Company) on the Nickel Plate Road.

It was a beautiful day across the fields of Indiana, the sun streaming through Matty's window. As he turned the page, he noticed that the train seemed to be slowing, the noise of steel and steam seemingly awakened.

"Next stop, Fort Wayne," blared the conductor.

By instinct, Christy lowered his shade as the train came to a halt, the famous hurler barely sensing the large crowd that was gawking on the depot platform.

"Do you see him?" wondered a curious fan. "Is this the train with the Giants?"

"He must be on there," said someone else. "I don't see him."

They looked, strained, and wondered. Where was the Great Mathewson?

And then the train methodically pulled away, building to full steam. A mile down the track, Matty's shade once again lifted.

Christy always drew huge crowds.

Hard work, sportsmanship, honesty, moral values, muscular Christianity . . . these were qualities of one Frank Merriwell, an enormously admired fictional character created by Gilbert Patten in 1896 for *Tip Top Weekly*. The Frank Merriwell series became so popular that it was soon a staple of the dime novel. The main character was the All-American Boy . . . athletic, intelligent, and forever getting ambushed at the edge of disaster . . . somehow finding a way to survive, to win . . . fair and square, of course. "He's a regular Frank Merriwell" was a common description for a person who practiced good sportsmanship.

Without a doubt, that would define Christopher Mathewson. The newspapers simply called him Matty, The Great Mathewson, The

Christian Gentleman, or Big Six . . . a comparison to New York's famous "Big Six" fire wagon that was built to rescue. Originally penned by Sam Crane – a sportswriter who had played second base for the Giants back in 1890 – the nickname stuck. A few even called Christy "Old Gumboots" for his knock-kneed stride.

As a child, Arthur Daley – a future columnist for the *New York Times* – got to see his first baseball game, the Giants with Matty pitching:

> "To a kid growing up in New York, the now legendary Big Six was a god. He was a big, handsome man with a picture book delivery. So smooth was his pitching motion that he lulled batters into a false sense of security. He just seemed to lob the ball to the plate, yet it was past them before they could get their bats around."

The legend of Matty would flourish in a world where communication mostly traveled by newspapers and word of mouth. While stories were usually based on truth, they could also carry a good dose of folklore. Sportswriters reported the facts . . . and then some.

According to Frank Graham of the *New York Herald*, Matty was the "Greek god in flannels," embellished by writers "not only as the almost perfect pitcher, but as the practically perfect man."

Grantland Rice called Christy a "symbol of clean, square, hard fighting sport with the determination to be just a plain, natural, regular fellow."

"Added to the wonderful arm and alert brain," wrote Harry Daniel, "there is a powerful man who is strong within himself."

As fact and fiction harmoniously weaved through the palate of Americana, Matty became the idol of men, women, and children. He was handsome, athletically gifted, virtuous, distinguished, impeccably dressed, clean cut, unique . . . absolutely no one on earth carried such an indisputably perfect image.

These were the known ingredients: Christy Mathewson was an extremely smart and clean-living small-town farm boy from Northeast Pennsylvania who went off to Bucknell where he excelled in academics and three sports. My goodness, he was an All-America football player and class president and member of two literary societies. He was tall, stunningly handsome, and muscular – both competitor and sportsman. Polite, honest, well spoken – he loved and respected his parents. Sound mind, body, and character – he was the definition of muscular Christianity. Didn't he make a promise to his mother that he would never play baseball on Sunday?

As with any legend, many of the details surrounding Matty's life were enhanced with a harmless measure of illusion: no liquor, no tobacco, no vulgarity . . . absolute purity of heart and mind . . . the emblem of all that is good and honest . . . a brilliant man who single-handedly brought dignity and sportsmanship to baseball, lifting the game from the dregs of vice to the summit of integrity.

First, Matty was not perfect.

"He smoked cigars, cigarettes, and a pipe," said sportswriter Frank Graham. "He was no drinker in the broad sense of the term, but he knew the difference between Scotch and Rye."

While Matty would never bet on baseball, he had a passion for gambling. He could remember cards and outsmart most any opposition, particularly knucklehead ballplayers. McGraw once fined him the astronomical sum of $500 for playing high-stakes poker with teammates.

"It's unfair," said the manager, "because Matty will always win and take their money and he knows it."

Christy countered, "You wonder how a man who had been so much to me, and I to him, could do such a thing. But he not only fined me $500, he made it stick. I never got it back."

The players, naturally, knew plenty about Christy . . . he was not quite as spotless as the public poster boy.

"Matty loved to gamble," said teammate Rube Marquard. "If you had a dollar in your pocket, he would never be satisfied until he got that dollar from you."

By the way, the Giants of 1905 adored Mathewson. After all, this was an entirely different clubhouse than the one he entered four years earlier. To toss out a worn football analogy, McGraw had opened the hole and all Christy had to do was head for daylight, which he did with great maturity and sincerity, earning respect by giving respect.

CHAPTER EIGHT

Laughing Larry Doyle, one of Matty's best friends, once said, "We were a rough, tough lot in those days. All except Matty. But he was no namby-pamby. He'd gamble, play cards, curse now and then and take a drink now and then. But he was always quiet and had a lot of dignity."

Writer Frank DeFord, in *The Old Ball Game*, offered a seamless insight. "The public thought Matty was faultless, while those who knew him thought he was wonderfully human."

To the fans, Big Six could do no wrong and nothing could possibly demean his status . . . even when he occasionally did blunder.

In July 1905, the Giants and Phillies instigated a near riot at Philadelphia's Baker Bowl as a brawl between players was joined by a scattered contingent of less-than-sober fans. When a teen-aged lemonade vendor rushed onto the field to join the mayhem, he was decked . . . by Christy Mathewson. But, even scandal could not soil Matty's image, the Philadelphia papers figuring "McGraw's venon had rubbed off on even Matty."

Like a train on a golden track, Matty's popularity could not be derailed. He was the good guy. Had he claimed even the slightest imperfection, the fans would simply counter that he was being modest.

Some narratives were absolutely true. "Did you know that Matty was an honor student at Bucknell?"

Some accounts were a stretch. "Do you realize that Matty has never once argued an umpire's call?"

And some were downright fables. "Did you hear that Matty once dropkicked a football 75 yards right through the middle of the goal post?"

As the tales were passed around the cities, towns, and farmlands (the nation was two-thirds rural), the rapidly escalating multitude of worshippers could not get enough. Didn't matter that most had never actually seen him, they knew all about Big Six . . . The Christian Gentleman . . . Matty . . . Old Gumboots . . . all within a world of no radio, no television, and no instant replay.

The story goes that Matty was sliding into home plate with the winning run. The play was close, the hard (but clean) slide kicking so much dust into the air that the umpire lost view of the tag. Not knowing if

Matty was safe or out, the ump looked into the Great Mathewson's eyes.

"He got me," said Matty, the umpire then lifting his fist to signal "out" as the Polo Grounds crowd gasped in shock.

"Why would you do that?" the opposing catcher asked.

"Because," said Matty, "I'm a church elder."

Was Matty a regular Frank Merriwell or Merriwell a regular Christy Mathewson? Whatever, Matty was christened the role model for all boys, the matinee superhero, a beacon of virtue leading the nation down a righteous path.

While his image personified muscular Christianity, Matty was never a preacher.

"He staunchly refused to let his teammates drag him down to their level," wrote sportswriter Fred Lieb. "By the force of his example and character, he lifted them up toward him until he was the most admired and respected man on the squad."

Matty possessed a "spiritual energy" and followed the Golden Rule without fault, proudly representing a wholesome ethical code that he learned from his parents and Pastor Harris at the old Factoryville First Baptist Church.

Except for the Sundays that he was on a train, Matty always attended church, at home with Jane or on the road by himself. He kept his bible close and even taught Sunday School.

"Mathewson was steady as a rock," said Damon Runyan, "a man of high morality and restraint, a preacher by word and precept of decent living."

How exactly it all unfolded was beyond him. Matty didn't court the spotlight as much as it fell on him. And if fame was thrown his way, why duck? The best explanation is that he walked into the perfect moment; the game desperately needed a hero and America took notice . . . right place, right time . . . celebrity just happened and off it went.

Although he was often astonished at the scope of adoration, he realized his good fortune. He knew the nation's perception and did not want to disappoint. Plus, it was basically true because even the myths defined his values. He was a good person who believed in a wholesome lifestyle and always tried to follow his moral compass. He loved the game, the tributes, and the glory. Best of all, he truly cherished being a role model.

"I feel strongly that it is my duty to show youth the good, clean, honest values that I was taught by my mother," he said. "That really is all I can do."

Even so, Christy was a bit uneasy about expectations, always coveting his privacy. Remember, behind the artist on the baseball diamond at times still lingered a quiet, discreet, and reserved kid.

"I owe everything I have to the fans when I am out there on the mound," he said, "but I owe the fans nothing when I am not pitching."

Then again, it was not within Christy's countenance to be rude.

"I remember how fans would constantly rush up to him and pester him with questions," said Laughing Larry Doyle, Matty's road roommate for several summers. "He hated it, but he was always courteous. I never saw a man who could shake off those bugs so slick without hurting their feelings."

In 1905, Matty completed his third straight season of cracking 30 wins, leading the league in victories (31-9), earned run average (1.28), strikeouts (206), and shutouts (8). He completed 32 of 37 starts and only allowed 64 walks in 339 innings. Where he had once heaved a league-worst 58 wild pitches from 1901-03, he only let six get out of the bag the entire summer.

And this year there would be a World Series. The Giants finished 105-48, far ahead of the Pirates and the dynasty-in-the-making Cubs. Their opponents in the first "official" Fall Classic would be Connie Mack's Philadelphia Athletics, loaded with talent and heavily favored by the sportswriters.

For the first game in Philly – the city where Matty had leveled the Lemonade Kid in July – Connie Mack bought his players new uniforms with a clever logo, in direct reference to a slanderous remark by John McGraw that the Athletics played like a "bunch of white elephants." The A's would need more than a nifty emblem. Mathewson would pitch three games in six days and win them all by shutouts . . . 27 scoreless innings.

He notched 18 strikeouts and only allowed 14 hits. In the negative column, there was one walk.

"I was so proud of my young husband," said Jane. "He then was 25 and already a nation's idol, but to me, he still was that big, good-looking boy from Bucknell."

Roger Bresnahan, who caught Matty's masterpieces, hit a dazzling .313 from the leadoff spot. The entire band of Giants got to slice up the winner's share for a hefty bonus of $1,141 per player, about a third of the average salary for an entire season. Plus, each player was awarded a diamond-studded gold button to commemorate the world victory.

According to the *New York Times,* in its sold-out edition of October 15, the moment was owned by Matty:

> "Philadelphia tried its best, but it was only a shadow reflecting the masterful Mathewson's will. He bestrode the field like a mighty Colossus, and the Athletics peeped about the diamond like pigmies who struggled gallantly for their lives, but in vain.
>
> Christie Mathewson, the giant slabman, may be legitimately designated as the pitching marvel of the century."

The supreme coronation had taken place less than an hour after Matty's third shutout sealed the crown. Late afternoon shadows had already begun to darken the Polo Grounds, but most of the jubilant crowd of 27,000 rooters still surrounded the centerfield entrance to the Giants' locker room, demanding their heroes step out onto the veranda. After McGraw had pushed the crowd into a frenzied state of euphoria, Matty appeared with Bresnahan, unfurling a large impromptu banner that read, "THE GIANTS, WORLD'S CHAMPIONS, 1905."

Matty would thank the crowd for their kindness, but graciously remind everyone that all of the other Giants were just as magnificent.

They weren't buying it . . . the Great One had thrown three straight shutouts, for heaven's sake . . . the Christian Gentleman was just being humble . . . again.

To those fans and millions across the nation, the 1905 World Series seemed to ensure that Matty's greatness and popularity just might last forever.

CHAPTER NINE

Late 1906 . . . New York City

A young boy gazed up from his crib, two beautiful faces smiling over him . . . softly whispering . . . a song in the background that was gentle and warm . . .

And the world was perfect . . .

On April 18, 1906, the San Francisco earthquake and subsequent fire killed more than 3,000 people, the worst natural disaster in the history of California. While major league baseball put together a string of exhibitions to help the city and its Pacific Coast League baseball team, the Seals, New Yorkers also were greatly concerned about the health of Christy Mathewson, slowly recovering from a frightening, near fatal bout of diphtheria.

With Jane expecting and Christy quarantined, friends were torn with worry. For John McGraw, it revived a horrible memory from his childhood. In 1885, just 12 years old, McGraw lost his mother, two sisters, and two brothers when a diphtheria outbreak struck Truxton, New York. Two decades later, he was once again distraught.

Big Six would be back in the box on May 5, wearing the Giants' new black uniform with "World Champions" in large white letters across the chest. Having already missed a month and not fully recovered, Matty managed seven good innings against Boston, but did not pitch again for nine days. Physically weak through July, he somehow managed to produce a stellar 22-12 record. But even a healthy Mathewson would not have fazed the mighty Cubs, the second-place Giants 20 games back.

Jane and Christy Jr.

But as soon as the season ended, baseball hardly mattered. On October 19, Christy Mathewson Jr. was born, a world of fans celebrating the wonderful event.

"He was a fat and chubby boy with light hair and blue eyes," said Blanche McGraw. "He was quite handsome."

Aunt Blanche and Uncle John were Sonny's extra set of parents. He was, after all, the child they had never had and they would spoil him accordingly, as would the stream of relatives from Lewisburg and Factoryville.

Now charged with raising a family, the Mathewsons decided to find a home of their own. Travel was fast and easy with the new subway system, but Christy and Jane found a large apartment in Washington Heights with a view of the Polo Grounds.

While Christy fretted over his son's every sniffle or cough, Jane had the maternal instincts of a woman raised in a large and caring family. The beautiful baby was strong, healthy, and coordinated. His first attempt at walking resulted in a dozen steps across the dining room floor . . . a curiosity born for adventure.

Christy kept politics at a distance, but he did admire Theodore Roosevelt, the old Rough Rider winning a second presidential election in 1906 while leading a progressive surge in America. Roosevelt's foreign policy underscored America's rise as a world superpower – the Panama Canal, the Monroe Doctrine, the Great White Fleet. On the domestic front, Roosevelt fought political corruption and corporate greed, his trust-busting "Square Deal" attempting to level the economic playing field for all Americans.

What really caught Christy's attention was Roosevelt's love of conservation, creating five national parks and 150 national forests on 230 million acres of unspoiled land. Like Matty, the nation's 26th president pushed the strenuous life, believing in a healthy body and moral mind. Roosevelt exercised, boxed, rowed, hiked, hunted, rode horses, and played tennis.

There were problems in America and Roosevelt had the ideas and energy to fix them . . . better times were certainly ahead.

John McGraw routinely surmised that the curse of marriage was that it ushered newlywed ballplayers into a one-year slump. Naturally, Matty had been an exception, notching his first 30-win season after his honeymoon in '03. But, would Big Six be able to escape the trials and repercussion of being a new father? No problem, he went 24-12 for the 1907 season with a 2.00 ERA, topping the league in wins, shutouts, and strikeouts. Unfortunately, it was the entire team that slumped, tumbling to fourth place as the runaway Cubs nabbed their second straight pennant before sweeping Ty Cobb and the Detroit Tigers in the World Series.

What quietly irritated Matty about '07 was that his brother, Henry, had been sent down to the minors. Taller and skinnier than his older brother, Henry had graduated from Bucknell in the spring of '06 and immediately signed with New York. Henry was 20 years old, and as it turned out, not quite ready for the big time. He earned a save in his initial appearance with the Giants, but his first start was a disaster, walking a record 14 Boston batters while getting shelled.

Shipped to Wilmington, Henry would never return to the majors, clipped with a career record of 0-1. Still, there was a third brother throwing strikes on the horizon. Only in high school, Nick Mathewson just might be the best pitcher in the family.

Roger "The Duke of Tralee" Bresnahan – Matty's catcher for four seasons – was a future Hall of Famer with bat, brains, and a turbulent temper. According to one sportswriter, Bresnahan was "highly strung and almost abnormally emotional." But off the field, like McGraw, Bresnahan was easy natured and considerate.

In 1907, Bresnahan became the first catcher to wear shin guards, a self-designed over-stuffed contraption resembling the leg pads of cricket. Matty thought the idea splendid. However, most everyone else trashed Bresnahan's innovation as cowardice. Pittsburgh manager Fred Clarke protested that the pads were a danger to sliding runners.

Still, Bresnahan was far from finished with his campaign for workplace safety. After being plunked by a bean ball, he stepped to the plate wearing protective headgear that closely matched a leather football helmet.

Two weeks before his death in 1934, John McGraw provided the *Sporting News* with his Top 50 pitching-catching combinations of all time. At the top of his list was the tandem of Christy Mathewson and Roger Bresnahan.

"Matty never had an equal, particularly in a pinch," said Bresnahan. "He was an absolute master . . . the greatest pitcher of all time."

In 1908, Mathewson and Bresnahan were robbed of certain victory in the most controversial game ever played.

With the season nearly over, three teams – Giants, Cubs, and Pirates – were locked in a dead even race for the pennant. On September 23 at the Polo Grounds, an anxious crowd of 30,000 cranks did not quite realize they were about to "participate" in history.

Big Six and Chicago's Jack Pheister had both pitched masterpieces. But, with two outs in the bottom of the ninth inning, Pheister was thrust into a nasty pinch after New York's Freddie Merkle, a 19-year-old rookie getting his first major-league start, singled Harry "Moose" McCormick to third with the potential winning run. Al Bridwell then put what should have been a major dent in the Cubs pennant hopes with a solid shot to center, sending McCormick home and the jubilant New York fans racing across the field, which was common in those days because the main exit of the Polo Grounds was in centerfield.

McCormick (winning run) and Bridwell (game-winning hit) were both mobbed by teammates and fans. Meanwhile, Merkle had pulled up 15 feet from the second base bag to celebrate and rushed to the centerfield locker room, a habit precipitated by the exuberance of fans on the field. Now, according to a strict interpretation of the rules, a runner must proceed safely to the next base to avert a force out. However, those who had read the rulebook considered it applying only to infield grounders, not a clear single to the outfield. Plus, the obscure rule had never been enforced.

With half the rooters now on the field celebrating, Chicago second baseman Johnny "The Crab" Evers – a student of the rulebook – began shouting to his centerfielder, Circus Solly Hoffman, to retrieve and throw the baseball. In Evers' mind, if Merkle is forced out at second, then the inning is over and McCormick's run doesn't count.

Iron Man McGinnity, who had been coaching first base for the Giants, noticed what Evers was doing as Hoffman worked his way through the outfield crowd to retrieve the ball. Matty, also seeing the sudden commotion, grabbed Merkle to get him safely to second. On the way, however, he asked the field umpire, Bob Emslie, if Merkle needed to tag. "No problem," said the ump. "You win the game."

The Cubs sure didn't think it was over, nor did McGinnity, now running full speed toward Evers at second. At 125 pounds, Evers was the smallest man on the field and Iron Man, remember, was a 206-pound former muleskinner. As the ball finally arrived from Circus Solly, so did the Iron Man, plowing into Evers with the full force of a middle linebacker. Needless to say, McGinnity won dibs on the ball and threw it as far as he could into the stands.

By this time, home plate umpire Hank O'Day had made his way to second, the two officials observing the heightened confusion.

According to one of the more popular versions of the incident, a reserve player on the Cubs, Floyd Kroh, went into the stands to request the ball back from a tall, middle-aged fan wearing a brown bowler hat. But the man refused to hand over the baseball.

"Kroh hit the man on top of the head," said Evers, "knocking the bowler over his eyes."

Stealing the ball from the blinded rooter, Kroh heaved it to Joe Tinker for the relay to Evers, who now tagged second, prize to the sky so that Umpire O'Day could take note.

O'Day could have easily walked away, but the exact same thing had happened under his watch several weeks earlier with the Cubs. When one of the Pirates didn't touch second, Evers stomped on second, unsuccessfully demanding that the winning run be negated. When O'Day decided the Pirates had won the game, the always high-strung Evers blasted him for choosing tradition over a rule that was right there, somewhere, in the book.

Not that O'Day was afraid of getting chewed out by Evers, who paraded an ego and vocabulary that could rival McGraw, but the obscure rule was still fresh in the ump's mind.

As both sides argued frantically to O'Day and Emslie, the hundreds of fans still milling on the now darkened field vigorously joined the home team's cause . . . leading to a near riot and an emergency umpire evacuation under police protection.

"There was hell a-poppin'," said Evers. "There must have been five fist fights going on as we finally got out of there."

Later that evening, O'Day decided that Merkle did not touch second – even though neither umpire saw the entire play – and, therefore, the winning run did not score. O'Day ruled the game a tie.

"It was a terrible thing to have happened," said Merkle. "I wished that a large hole would open up and swallow me."

Fueled over the years by a thousand different versions of the same event, what exactly happened has been lost to history. Some say Chicago first baseman (and manager) Frank Chance grabbed another baseball from the Cubs dugout and personally took it to second where he ceremoniously stomped on the bag. Another twist was that Merkle actually came back and touched second while McGinnity was pummeling Evers.

The next day in the *New York Times*, sportswriter W.W. Aulick wrote that, "Merkle's bonehead play was the dumbest mistake ever made by a player."

Aulick was witnessing history:

> "Bridwell hits safely to centre, McCormick trots home. The reporter boys prepare to make an asterisk under the box score of the game with the line, two out when winning run was scored. The merry villagers flock on the field to worship the hollow where the Mathewson feet have pressed, and all of a sudden there is a doings around second base. And then begins the argument which will keep us in talk for the rest of the season, and then some."

Again, don't blame Matty . . .

"From a spectacular point of view, that mix-up at the finish was just the appropriate sensation to a bang-up, all-a-quiver game. Up to the climactic ninth it was the toss of a coin who would win. For here is our best-beloved Mathewson pitching as only champions pitch, striking out the power and the glory of the Cubs."

The entire matter might have tumbled into obscurity but for one circumstance. Sure enough, after a wild scramble with the Pirates exiting on the final day of the regular season, the Giants and Cubs were deadlocked in first. The tie game would need to be replayed. That would occur on October 8 at the Polo Grounds, a one-game playoff with the winner to face the Detroit Tigers in the World Series.

The Giants were furious, some of the players wanting to boycott the game. They still believed they had won the original game and that the Cubs had only been rewarded for a technicality. A large group of New Yorkers found out what hotel the Cubs were staying in and spent the entire night before the game honking horns, yelling, and doing anything possible to keep the Chicago players from sleeping.

However, it was the Giants who were hurting. Roger Bresnahan (sciatic rheumatism), Mike Donlin (muscle spasms), and Fred Tenney (two hamstrings) should not have been playing. Larry Doyle was badly spiked and had just gotten out of the hospital.

"How are the cripples?" McGraw bellowed as the players arrived to the ballpark. "Any more to add to the list of identified dead?"

And then there was Freddie Merkle.

"He was drawn up in the corner of the bench, pulling away from us as if he had some contagious disease," said Christy. "We tried to cheer him up, but he was inconsolable."

During the stretch run for the pennant, Christy had pitched nine times in two weeks and thrown nearly 400 innings for the season. His arm felt heavy and stiff. Before heading to the park on October 8, he told Jane, "I'm not fit to pitch today."

She gave him a hug and kiss, encouraging him to do his best. She also wanted him to remember that she and Sonny would be at the park cheering.

Newspapers reported that as many as 250,000 people tried to storm the Polo Grounds for the one-game playoff. Since only 40,000 people could possibly fit into the stadium, those who were turned away charged up Coogan's Bluff to watch from the outfield. Hundreds were injured in a stampede. Even Jane and two-year-old Sonny were nearly crushed, pulled from the crowd by a policeman. Two fans fell to their death from the elevated train track.

There was even a rumor that Fred Merkle had killed himself.

Meanwhile, the Cubs couldn't get into the stadium – policemen had revolvers drawn to escort them through the gates while firemen used high-powered hoses to turn away those trying to scale the walls.

On the field, Frank Chance punched Iron Man McGinnity in the jaw, instigating a bench-clearing, pregame fistfight. Later, Chance would suffer a ruptured cartilage in his neck, hit by a flying pop bottle from the stands. Catcher Johnny Kling would snag a foul pop-up in "a shower of beer bottles."

Said Chicago pitcher Three-Finger Brown, "The Polo Grounds was the closest to a lunatic asylum as any place I've ever seen."

Long story short, the Giants lost 4-2, Brown earning the victory in relief.

"I never had less on the ball in my life," said Matty.

The season in ashes, John Brush presented each of his players with a medal . . . "The Real Champions, 1908."

As for Merkle – now and forevermore known as "Bonehead" and "Wrong Way" – he was ruthlessly razzed by fans and haunted by the incident for the remainder of his life. "Hey Bonehead, don't forget to touch second," the cranks would holler from the stands.

"When I die," he would say late in life, "I guess they'll put on my tombstone, 'Here lies Bonehead Merkle.'"

But McGraw and the Giants always stood strong in Merkle's defense.

"It is criminal to say that Merkle is stupid and to blame the loss of the pennant on him," said McGraw. "In the first place, he is one of the smartest and best players on this ball club. In the second place, he didn't cost us the pennant. We lost a dozen games we should have won."

"It could have happened to anyone," said Matty. "There's no sense eating our hearts out."

Matty finished the 1908 season as the NL leader in victories (37), ERA (1.43), shutouts (11), complete games (34), saves (5), and strikeouts (259). In 390 innings, he allowed only 42 walks and threw but two wild pitches. Of course, what is remembered most is not that his record was 37-11, but that it should have been 38-10.

CHAPTER TEN

November 1908 . . . Washington Heights

Christy put down The Trail of the Lonesome Pine and closed his eyes. He was still caught in the '08 season, trying to dissect why it had ended so suddenly, the unforgiving injustice of sport.

For one innocent mistake, Fred Merkle had become the scourge of all mankind. It was all so absurd.

Matty pictured the fateful moment that McCormick scored and the game was won, but then the commotion. All Freddie had to do was run another 15 feet . . . Christy could have even pushed him to second base.

"You have to touch second, Freddie. It's somewhere in the rulebook. Okay, it's never been called until now, but it's still a rule. Just touch the bag."

A few more steps and none of this would have happened . . .

Or if McGraw had only switched Merkle and Moose McCormick in the batting order . . . Freddie would have been on third and scored, Moose certainly would have touched second.

"Whoa, the Giants might be world champs," his thoughts continued, picturing the acceptance of another trophy. "We would have crushed Detroit."

Christy snapped back to reality. Whatever might have been, Freddie did not deserve the cruelty that was still being thrown by the newspapers and cranks. Matty, McGraw, and most of the team had tried to console poor Merkle. The kid was emotionally destroyed and it wasn't fair.

Opening his eyes, Matty glanced at Jane, reading the latest issue of *Collier's Weekly.* He paused, wondering what might be going through her mind. She undoubtedly was not thinking about how badly the Giants had been wronged.

Climbing over his mother, Sonny was playing with his wooden airplane . . . two years old and happily buzzing around the room as if he ruled the universe.

A moment in time . . .

It might have appeared that Harry "Moose" McCormick was trying to shadow Matty. Two years younger, Moose became the fullback on the Bison football team when Matty left school. He played baseball, basketball, and was even a member of Matty's fraternity, Phi Gamma Delta. After graduating from Bucknell in 1904, Moose would become a decent major-league outfielder and baseball's first pinch-hitting specialist . . . one more college kid jumping into the fray.

Before Christy hit the big leagues, few college athletes sought professional baseball careers. In 1868, the legendary Cap Anson spent one semester at the University of Iowa before being asked to leave due to "behavior" difficulties. During McGraw's playing days, he and Hughie Jennings attended St. Bonaventure during the offseason, Jennings later studying law at Cornell. John Montgomery Ward – who pitched a perfect game in the summer of Christy's birth – graduated from Penn State and Columbia Law.

Bucknell's first pro player was Harold "Hal" McClure, an outstanding catcher who played for the Boston Red Caps in 1882. McClure had graduated from Bucknell in 1877 and played minor league baseball from Philadelphia to Rochester while earning a master's degree. He played two games in the majors with two singles in six plate appearances before deciding to study law. Extremely intelligent and modest, McClure would eventually become one of the youngest judges in Pennsylvania, described as a man "with pure life and correct ideals." The McClure family lived in a beautiful home on the edge of the Bucknell campus and became good friends with the Mathewsons.

Ward, Jennings, and McClure were exceptions. Overall, pro baseball at the turn of the century still subscribed to the hard knocks of life, its players usually ranging from slightly educated to downright illiterate. Players made little money, had no security, and were generally regarded as derelicts and thugs. The image was so tarnished that teams were often denied lodging at even the shabbiest of hotels.

The rise of the American League, cleaner standards, better pay, and the national love affair with Christy Mathewson opened a new door for the scholar-athlete. Suddenly, a career playing baseball was socially acceptable and encouraged. By the 1920s, roughly one-third of all pro players would have college backgrounds.

Bucknell was a baseball factory in the first decade after Matty left school, sending 14 more players to the majors. McCormick and Sandy Piez both teamed with Matty on the Giants. Even though they were on the cross-town New York Highlanders, Walter Blair and Bert Daniels were good friends with the Mathewsons. Bucknell would send Jimmy Sebring and Bucky Veil to the Pirates, Jim Clark and Dick Kauffman to St. Louis. The Philadelphia Athletics had Dean Sturgis and Weldon Wyckoff from Bucknell, while the Phillies grabbed Mickey "Doc" Doolan. Jiggs Parson and Jake "Jerky" Northrop would play for the Boston Braves.

The Giants had a fair share of college boys. Third baseman Art Devlin had graduated from Georgetown, outfielder Fred Snodgrass from St. Vincent's College in California (now Loyola Marymount). Jack "Chief" Meyers attended Dartmouth, Fred Tenney had gone to Brown, and Eddie Grant – the first ballplayer killed in action during World War I – had earned undergraduate and law degrees at Harvard.

Across the league, there was Eddie Collins (Columbia), George Sisler (Michigan) Jack Barry (Holy Cross), Jack Coombs (Colby), Pop Williams (Bowdoin), Bunny Hearn (Elon), Zeb Terry (Stanford), and Branch Rickey (Ohio Wesleyan), to name a few.

Meanwhile, intelligence and great quotes were a definite attraction for sportswriters, who also were often highly educated. There was Sam Crane (MIT), W.O. McGeehan (Stanford), Bozeman Bulger (Alabama), and Heywood Broun (Harvard).

Grantland Rice, a young sportswriter for the *Atlanta Journal* who had graduated from Vanderbilt, first met Matty at the 1905 World Series.

Both 25 years old with similar interests, they became great friends, non-stop competitors at cards, chess, and golf.

As did a younger Heywood Broun, who arrived at the *New York Morning Telegraph* with a reputation as a "card and checkers shark." John McGraw, certain the Harvard boy was about to be whittled down a few notches, set up a checkers game against Matty in the Giants' clubhouse. The Christian Gentleman took two of three.

"You're a very sound player," Matty told the rookie reporter. It was the beginning of many splendid battles.

Writers like Damon Runyon, Fred Lieb, and Ring Lardner may never have gone to college, but they loved a lively intellectual discussion. Matty, Chief Meyers, "Harvard Eddie" Grant . . . they'd gab from Pittsburgh to St. Louis if the reporter could stay awake.

"I can spend a lifetime writing about Matty," wrote Runyan, "and I shall know enough about Bucknell and other aspects of clean living to found a monastery."

It was well known within the Factoryville clan that Christy was not the best pitcher in his family. Sure, he was currently the best there ever was, but young Nicholas Mathewson would change all that. Ten years younger than Christy, Nick had been offered a lucrative contract out of high school to play for the Detroit Tigers. Gilbert Mathewson objected, urging his youngest son to first attend college. Christy concurred with his father.

"Now," Christy had written, "I would advise a boy who has exceptional ability as a ballplayer to sign no contracts and to take no money for playing until he has finished college."

In the fall of '08, Nick entered Lafayette College, near the New Jersey border in Easton. Home for Christmas vacation, he seemed no different than any other freshman . . . signs of slight homesickness, somewhat frazzled by his studies, and a touch distant . . . but everyone figured that he'd be fine . . . especially once baseball rolled around in the spring.

In January, after heading back to school, Nick unexpectedly returned to Factoryville. He went to the barn, wrote an unintelligible note, and shot himself. The following morning, the family – including Christy and Jane – were at his hospital bedside when he died, just 19 years old.

Their grief was deep, private . . .

About the time that Robert E. Peary was planting a flag on the North Pole, the Giants were holding spring training in Marlin, Texas, Christy Mathewson taking a line drive to the hand off the bat of Moose McCormick. Christy would miss nearly a month of the 1909 regular season, but was still dominant. After Matty pitched a 5-0 victory against the Cubs without allowing a walk, catcher Chief Meyers took no credit for the shutout.

"Anybody can catch Matty," said the rookie. "You could catch him sitting in a rocking chair."

Christy finished the year 25-6 with a career-best 1.14 ERA. Even so, the Pirates took the pennant with the hated Cubs in second and New York a distant third.

Major-league baseball had traveled far in the first decade of the century. Despite the old grudges and hatreds, the two leagues had found equal footing. It helped that baseball was a daily feature of every newspaper, a prime seat at the heart of American communications. Of course, New York led the nation with seven newspapers in the morning and six in the evening. Even the New York Central Railroad posted up-to-date final baseball scores in the smoking cars on all trains to Chicago and back.

It also enhanced professional baseball's progress that everyone was making money, attendance doubling and the value of an average franchise having increased tenfold in one decade. The $200,000 that John Brush invested to buy the Giants was bringing handsome returns, his profits averaging $100,000 per season. Even minor-league baseball was booming, expanding from 12 leagues in 1900 to 46 by 1912.

Without doubt, the game's resounding popularity was based on its long line of stars. Christy had some strong company at the top – Honus Wagner in Pittsburgh, Ty Cobb in Detroit, Cy Young in Boston, Three-Finger Brown in Chicago, Walter Johnson in Washington, to name but a few.

As might be expected, Matty greatly admired his peers, calling Cobb and Wagner "stars of the first magnitude, both doing their best work when pressed hardest."

The Christian Gentleman.

Matty had also seen action in one more "big game" during the summer of 1909, returning to Bucknell in June for the Alumni Game. While the varsity notched a 13-12 victory, Matty threw two innings, played an errorless third base, and collected three hits. Although one of the few alums without a degree, he was also the wealthiest, earning a monstrous 10 grand per year . . . and that was just for pitching.

Fully understanding the financial value of his popularity, Matty was a master of endorsements – Coca Cola, Blauvelt Sweaters, Arrow shirt collars, leg garters for socks, shaving razors, Tuxedo Chewing Tobacco. There also was the Christy Mathewson Parlor Baseball Game, for which he was paid $1,000 for endorsing plus two cents for every board game that was sold. It proved to be a blockbuster.

Christy starred in a silent movie, *The Umpire*, and co-wrote a Broadway play, *The Girl and the Pennant*. Along with his catcher, Chief Meyers, Matty was even a vaudeville headliner at the Fifth Avenue Theatre. Seventh on the program of a dozen acts with two performances daily, *Curves* also featured May Tully, who co-wrote the production with sportswriter Bozeman Bulger. Mathewson was billed as "the peerless pitcher" and Meyers "the Indian backstop."

Acting was definitely not Christy's passion, just a vehicle to somehow overcome an awkward shyness.

"He was conscious, and annoyed, that many people thought his timidity was arrogance or swell-headedness," said Bulger. "He hadn't that knack of making pleasant conversation upon meeting strangers and he struggled hard to overcome it. So he went on the stage for the sole purpose of training himself to feel at ease in making public talks and in addressing strangers. When he appeared ill at ease and non-communicative, it hurt him worse than the person he was addressing."

The training worked. When he wasn't barnstorming or visiting California with Jane and Sonny, Christy established an extremely successful insurance business, not to mention Jane's input on the stock market.

Matty's name equaled money. But he did maintain principles. In fact, several wealthy businessmen proposed the creation of a drinking establishment called "The Christy Mathewson." All he had to do was show up for a few minutes a week to shake hands and he would earn thousands of dollars per year. He declined the offer.

"Money can cost too much," said Minerva Mathewson. "He told me, 'Mother, if I had to make money that way I wouldn't want any.' Christy knows there is something in the world worth more than money."

As did Jane: "All the money in the world would not pay to have my husband away from his home all the time."

Financially, the Mathewsons were doing just fine . . . and, forever, very much in love.

To fulfill another aspiration, Matty began writing children's books with sportswriter W.W. Aulick – *Second Base Sloan, Catcher Craig, Pitcher Pollock, First Base Faulkner* . . .

And, with ghostwriter John Wheeler, he penned baseball books for all ages – *Won In The Ninth, Pitching In A Pinch*. Christy also co-wrote *The Battle of Base-Ball*.

Sportswriter Bozeman Bulger ghostwrote many of Christy's newspaper and magazine articles.

"He was very interested in the writer's life," said Bulger, who often roomed with Matty on train trips.

But life for The Christian Gentleman went far beyond work and money. He could shoot a round of golf in the low eighties. He was consumed with horticulture, reading, puzzles, and games . . . bridge, whist, poker, chess, and checkers.

After the 1909 season, the three Mathewsons were headed by train for California, but first made a stop in Texas. Matty had agreed to a three-week "barnstorming" contract to pitch for the El Paso White Sox. The club even brought in Jimmy Archer of the Chicago Cubs, who was widely considered the finest defensive catcher in the game with a cannon for an arm.

On November 2, before a sellout crowd, Matty hurled a five-hitter as El Paso beat Morenci 10-3. He would go undefeated for the White Sox, but that was only part of his western saga.

"Mathewson Trims Checker Sharps" was the headline of the November 12 edition of the *El Paso Herald*. At the local YMCA, Christy had opposed a dozen of the state's best checkers champs in a four-ring match. According to the *Herald*, Matty went undefeated while playing "three men at one time and taking them into camp as fast as they could move their men."

What did they expect? Christy Mathewson was second vice president of the American Checkers Association. He was known to defeat eight opponents at the same time . . . and, just to make it interesting, Matty would play blindfolded.

He probably could have pitched blindfolded.

"There is something about Mathewson – his bearing, his manner – that gives you the impression that you are going up against Gibraltar," said Eddie Collins, who had faced Matty in the 1905 World Series. "Why, at times it seemed he actually smiled at me."

"He knew exactly what you couldn't hit, and that was all you had to hit at," said Johnny Evers, "for he could throw a ball into a tin cup at pitching range."

CHAPTER ELEVEN

May 3, 1910 . . . Washington Heights

Christy was hiding behind the couch, three-year-old Sonny charging through the living room in yet another early morning adventure of hide-and-seek.

"Daddy, where are you?" Sonny jabbered, looking for the easy find. "You can tell me."

Christy remained quiet, hidden.

"Oh Daddy, where are you?" came the mimic from Jane's voice, not one to usually join the hunt. "Oh, look Sonny, do I see someone hiding behind the couch?"

Christy heard the quick approach of footsteps and giggles.

"Got you Daddy," squealed Sonny as he jumped on Christy, the two rolling happily on the floor.

"May I speak with you, Daddy?" came a stern command from Jane, Christy having no idea what he might have done wrong.

Standing, he saw Jane with a copy of the *New York Times*.

"Yesterday afternoon," she said, "I asked you how things went in Brooklyn? You said, and I quote, 'fine, I pitched a one-hit shutout.' And, like always, I believed you."

Christy was puzzled.

"Well?"

"Well," she interrupted, "You lied to me Christopher Mathewson. You promised to always tell the truth and you lied."

And then she smiled, turning the sports page of the *Times* in his direction, the headline reading, "Brooklyn Gets No-Hit by Mathewson."

"A no-hitter, Christy?" she continued. "You didn't even know you pitched a no-hitter?"

"I didn't," he countered. "They had a grounder in the eighth that Art Devlin grabbed and threw low. We all thought it was an error, but the scorekeeper called it a hit."

"Are you sure?"

"Yes, I was pitching. The official scorekeeper called it a hit. It was a one-hitter."

"So, then, you're saying the *New York Times* is lying to the entire city?"

"It appears so," he confessed with a sly grin.

Jane's smile turned to laughter as she playfully smacked him with the sports page.

"Christy Dear," she added, "you are loved way too much in this town."

And this was true.

On May 2, 1910 at Brooklyn's Washington Park, Christy won his third game of the young season with a 6-0 victory. The only hit by the Superbas occurred in the eighth inning when Pryor McElveen slapped a routine grounder toward short that third sacker Art Devlin cut off and threw errantly into the dirt at first. Art, Christy, Muggsy, and the rest of the Giants assumed it was an error, but the scorekeeper called it a hit.

The *New York Times* agreed with the Giants, reporting that Devlin's throw WAS an error. The banner headline and story proclaimed the pitching gem:

> "There are those in Brooklyn today who will say that Matty was found for a single by McElveen in the eighth. An untimely play by Arthur Devlin, which resulted in an error, was the only performance of the whole game that cast a blemish on the flinging of the big boxman."

The *Times* printed the box score with no hits and put a rub on any Giants' fan missing the game.

> "The wiseacres who stayed on the side of the river yesterday and cackled up their sleeves at their friends for going way over to Brooklyn to see a ball game read the bulletin boards last night with their orbs popping out of their heads. They are sorry they didn't go."

Unfortunately for Matty and the *Times*, the official major-league record book lists the feat as a one-hitter.

Christy and Sonny were quite close.

During his career, Matty would pitch two no-hitters (St. Louis 1901 and Chicago 1905). He would notch four one-hitters, the last being the 1910 Brooklyn game. From 1904-08, he beat the Cardinals 24 straight times. He earned 22 consecutive wins over Cincinnati (1908-11).

Along with healthy living and careful training, there were secrets to Matty's success.

"First control, second knowledge, and third ability," he said. "And through it all is the great factor of luck."

The cerebral pitcher played his game to precision.

"Here was a man with pinpoint control," wrote Arthur Daley, "a man who had all hitters' likes and dislikes so well catalogued that he was always pitching to weakness, never to strength."

"Matty was without peer," said John McGraw.

It would be a mistake to forget that Matty was also quite handsome. Male sportswriters could not help but describe his physique.

"He has the most magnificent shoulders you will find on any man," wrote Harry Daniel of the *Chicago Inter Ocean*.

Women definitely took notice. In April 1910, Kate Carew, who had never even seen a baseball game, interviewed Christy for the *New York American Journal*:

> "He was all in green – green clothes, green tie, green shirt, green socks – and his shoulders were ever so broad, and his eyes ever so blue, and his hair ever so yellow, and his cheeks ever so red, and I thought of Phoebus, the sun-god, and a young Viking with a sword . . . and, oh dear, the strength and gladness of youth were about him like a garment."

Did she mention that his large eyes were a "vivid rain-wash corn-flower blue?

Carew asked Big Six if it was "inconvenient to be so popular?"

"Oh no, I don't mind it a bit."

"But," she pressed, "don't you receive a great many letters from young ladies?"

"Mash notes? Oh yes," he said with a grin. "My wife answers those."

The 1910 season was routine for Matty, going a league-best 27-9 with a 1.89 ERA. He pitched 318 innings and had three times more strikeouts than walks. Still, the Cubs ran away with the pennant before falling to the Athletics in the World Series.

Did anyone in New York really care?

Size matters. According to the 1910 census, the only three cities in America with populations above a million were New York, Chicago, and Philadelphia. And, at 4.7 million residents, New York was still bigger than the other two combined. So big, that the Giants and New York Highlanders – both finishing second in their respective leagues – decided to hold a best-of-seven City Series. They didn't even bother to wait until the real World Series concluded.

The Manhattan Series would draw 103,033 fans, the Giants winning in six games over the Highlanders (a team the media was now calling the "Yankees"). In Game One, Mathewson would best rookie sensation Russell Ford and his "mysterious moist ball." A master of scuffing and wetting, Ford openly used an emery board in the box while winning 26 games. But, how the *Times* loved Matty.

> "Never have the local baseball-hungry thousands burst into such eruptions of deep-throated and shrill-voiced tribute as greeted Christy Mathewson when he mowed the Yankees down by the marvelous skill of his masterful pitching."

An interesting sidebar during the series was an incident at Hilltop Park, home of the Yankees. Giants' owner John T. Brush had parked his automobile inside the stadium by the right field wall, barely outside fair territory. When Yankees' outfielder Charlie Hemphill ripped a liner over Freddie Merkle's head at first, the extra base hit angled to the corner. Hemphill, who raced safely around the bases with what he expected must be an inside-the-park homer, was instead sent back to second by the umpires with a ground-rule double . . . it seems that the ball had gotten stuck under the owner's auto.

Matty would defeat the Highlanders three times during the postseason exhibition showdown, the winning Giants each pocketing $1,100 for the extra week of work.

CHAPTER TWELVE

Summer 1911 . . . Polo Grounds

Little Napoleon stood at the top of the dugout stairs, his arms folded, his eyes glaring, his entire body locked tight with a boiling rage . . .

There were three reasons the dynamite was smoldering . . . Hank O'Day was behind the plate, the evil Cubs were today's enemy, and an early Giants lead had completely vanished.

Big Six knew that McGraw was one twitch from explosion.

As always, the feisty coacher had been working the opposition since the opening pitch, zeroing in on any flaw, any attempt to distract an opponent's focus. The Cubs refused to bite. And, of course, the more Muggsy was ignored, the louder he became . . . and now his wrath was concentrated on Chicago's star twirler, Mordecai "Three Finger" Brown, who had arrived in relief to save the day . . .

As a child, Brown had lost two fingers in a farm machinery accident.

"Hey Brownie, you should stick your head in that whacker," McGraw yelled.

Muggsy also had the home cranks stirring, fueling the chorus of insults and bellyaching.

"C'mon you stupid ump, that wasn't even close," they bellowed at a pitch to Moose McCormick that might – or might not – have cut the corner of the plate. "Go back to Chicago, O'Day."

It was on . . .

Like an eagle on a rodent, McGraw sprung from the dugout with such fury that he had a hard time getting his expletives in order, randomly spitting words that made no sense outside of the moment.

Mathewson seldom listened to McGraw's rants, preferring to hear the pleasant music in his own head. But this was high theater, Muggsy screaming at O'Day with a clatter of piercing hysteria that actually drowned out the noise of 30,000 other whack jobs in the Polo Grounds.

Enjoying the ruckus, Freddie Merkle sat next to Mathewson.

"Sounds like shrieking thunder," laughed Merkle, a fleeting glance to the sky as if the very atmosphere might crack.

"Here it comes," said Matty, a split second before O'Day launched a hefty gesture of expulsion that would only drive McGraw – and the crowd – to a new level of insanity.

From the pitcher's box, Three Finger Brown glanced toward the New York dugout, briefly catching the eyes of his old pitching adversary, Christy Mathewson.

Brownie and Matty both smiled . . . just another day at the Polo Grounds.

Hank O'Day was a National League umpire for 30 years, most noted for disallowing Moose McCormick's winning run in the infamous 1908 "Bonehead Merkle" game between the Giants and Cubs. But O'Day would also be remembered as the only person in history to be a major-league player, manager, and umpire.

A flat face on a rugged frame, O'Day appeared grouchy and unapproachable. Matty once claimed to have actually seen O'Day laugh.

"His face acted as if it wasn't accustomed to the exercise and broke all in funny new wrinkles," said Matty, "like a glove when you put it on for the first time."

Whatever the stern appearance, O'Day was a man of unwavering integrity and a stickler for the rules. Or, as Matty put it, "stubborn and bullheaded."

Never an admirer of the umpire, John McGraw was well aware that O'Day was born and raised in Chicago, but skimmed past the fact that he had played two seasons for the New York Giants (1889-90). Obviously, O'Day was not a sympathetic sounding board for Little Napoleon.

"O'Day has to be handled with shock absorbers," said Christy. "McGraw tries to do it, but shock absorbers do not fit him well, and the first thing that usually occurs is a row."

Of course, McGraw never backed down. "Let me do the kicking," he would tell his players when O'Day was behind the plate. Time and again, guess who got the boot?

"It is as dangerous to argue with him," said Matty of O'Day, "as it is to try to ascertain how much gasoline is in the tank of an automobile by sticking down the lighted end of a cigar."

Under McGraw, the New York Giants always had an interesting dugout. First, he liked to collect ballplayers in his own image –rough and gritty scrappers like Art Devlin, Art Fletcher, Al Bridwell, Roger Bresnahan, and Fred Snodgrass – small in stature and busting with fight. They were brutal, fearless, and easily agitated.

"There was fighting everywhere they went," said sportswriter Frank Graham.

Naturally, Muggsy encouraged the mayhem.

"I got along with McGraw fine," said Bridwell. "He only suspended me once for two games. It was on account that I socked him."

But don't make the mistake of branding the Giants as a bunch of knuckleheads or misfits . . . it was an eclectic group.

Laughing Larry Doyle, a phenomenal hitter and good second sacker, had a vibrant personality, once commenting, "it's great to be young and a Giant."

John Tortes "Chief" Meyers took over as Matty's catcher after Bresnahan was traded to the Cardinals in 1909. A Native American from the Cahuilla tribe of Southern California, Meyers attended Dartmouth College before signing with the Giants. Meyers was smart, humorous, calm, and cultured. He visited art galleries in every city the team played, had a keen understanding of politics and philosophy, devotedly studied the art of hitting, and loved the theater.

Christy could nail a golf ball.

Despite that one "bonehead" play in 1908, Fred Merkle was an outstanding first sacker and team favorite. He once hooked Matty on golf, the pair often heading out for a quick morning round with Grantland Rice, Ring Lardner, and other sportswriters. When the Giants hit a midseason slump, McGraw pronounced the links off limits. Matty was miffed.

"I see no reason why a player's batting average should suffer from playing golf," he said. "The golf ball is much smaller. If anything, I should suppose that practice at hitting so small a sphere in exactly the way desired ought to be excellent experience for the batter."

But, Little Napoleon set the rules. Once, after Big Six lost an unfathomable three games in a row, McGraw ordered him to stop playing checkers.

Seemingly the hottest ticket in town, the Polo Grounds was a favorite hangout of actors, comedians, and the New York elite. Regulars included Will Rogers, W.C. Fields, Lillian Russell, Mabel Hite, Eddie Foy, May Tully, Digby Bell, and DeWolf Hopper ("Casey at the Bat"). George M. Cohan had season tickets, as did Gentleman Jim Corbett, the former heavyweight boxing champ turned stage actor. It was not uncommon to see John McCormack, the world-famous Irish tenor, or William Jay Gaynor, the mayor of New York, smiling for the crowd from their box seats.

Toward the end of the decade, the old wooden stadiums were replaced by gigantic' modern palaces of concrete and steel. In 1909, Philadelphia's Shibe Park had been built for half a million dollars and Pittsburgh's marvelous Forbes Field for nearly twice the money. Modern fireproof stadiums would include Chicago's Comiskey Park (1910) and Boston's Fenway Park (1912).

Squeezed in between was a new version of the Polo Grounds, much of its wooded structure having burned down on April 14, 1911. While the Yankees graciously rented Hilltop Park to the Giants for their home dates, John Brush oversaw a rapid reconstruction that had the Giants back on their field by the end of June, the expansive horseshoe-style Polo Grounds measuring 483 feet to straightaway center with a more reasonable distance down the corners. While the capacity would be 34,000 in 1911, it would be expanded to 55,000 in 1923.

Prior to every game, John McGraw loved to mingle with the celebrities, often waiting until the players actually took the field before getting into his baseball focus.

"New York has a much wider horizon than Factoryville," Christy once wrote, but he and his wife had no interest in chumming with the celebrities of Broadway, leaving the nightlife to John and Blanche.

According to the *New York Herald*, the big city can "kill a successful man by kindness. When repeated night after night, the muscles begin to sag, the fat grows, and the eyes are dimmed. Matty said 'No' to the very first invitation."

From actors to gamblers, businessmen to restaurateurs, it would have been easy for Matty and Jane to become swallowed by fame. Not a chance.

"In all of Manhattan," wrote a gossip columnist, "Matty is the hardest celebrity to find. That's because he's always home."

Not that the Mathewson's didn't have a welcome mat.

Christy cherished his teammates, and they him. Jack Meyers enjoyed many home-cooked meals at the Mathewson home, often playing bridge with Christy, Jane, and Freddie Merkle. Meyers once called "Bonehead" Merkle the smartest person on the team, no offense to Matty. That probably explains why Matty and Bonehead were bridge partners when the team was traveling.

Laughing Larry Doyle was Matty's road roommate. At the same time, Jane and Larry's wife, Gertrude, became good friends. Jane hung out with many of the wives. But, like her best friend, Blanche McGraw, many of the women seemed to have Broadway in their blood. Turkey Mike Donlin and Rube Marquard were both married to actresses, Mabel Hite and Blossom Seeley. Art Fletcher's wife was a high-society heiress, Irene Dieu.

Meanwhile, Christy had not strayed far from his old Bucknell fraternity brothers, often inviting them and their families to the Polo Grounds.

Lewis and Mary Theiss did not have far to travel. After graduating in 1902, Lewis Edwin Theiss joined the editorial staff of the *New York Sun*. At Bucknell, he had played on the varsity basketball team with Matty, but had made his athletic mark as captain of the Bison track and field squad, holding the school pole vault record for 12 years. While Matty was the class president in 1900-01, Lewis was voted to that post the following year.

Mary Bartol Theiss and Jane had been friends since childhood, both eventually attending the women's institute at Bucknell. Mary was now a freelance writer and women's suffragist.

In 1912, after a landmark parade down Fifth Avenue for women's suffrage, Jane commented to the press that she had "no doubt at all that it's a wonderfully good movement."

Other than a love for playing cards, there were plenty of interests and ties between the Theiss and Mathewson families. Mary's father, William

Cyrus Barton, had been Christy's math professor in college. While the women chatted about the old days in Lewisburg and raising their young children, the men talked horticulture. Christy was fascinated with the subject and Lewis was now the garden editor of two magazines, *Good Housekeeping* and *People's Home Journal*. He would eventually become head of the Bucknell Journalism department, by then one of the nation's leading authors of books for young men.

Lewis Theiss realized Matty's watershed contribution to baseball.

"It was because of his genuine sportsmanship, his integrity, his cleanness of life, his high ideals, that baseball was made over and raised to a cleaner, higher, level," wrote Theiss. "In all history, there is perhaps no more striking case of the force of a good example."

Along with wives and children, fraternity brothers' Ernest Sterling, Joe Davis, George English, and Karl Tiffany also were welcome guests of the Mathewsons, as was Bucknell president John Howard Harris and his wife, Lucy. Matty's old football coach, George "Doc" Hoskins, made regular visits to the Polo Grounds and Washington Heights.

There was a comforting grace about the Mathewson home, most days tranquil and unassuming. Then the relatives arrived from Lewisburg and Factoryville, or old college chums, business associates, ballplayers and their families. There was always plenty of room.

Besides being the same age, Matty and his catcher, Jack Meyers, had much in common . . . from reading to bridge, college football to the philosophy of life. Considering the time, it should be mentioned that they differed in heritage . . .

In the modern world of early 1900s, racism was matter-of-fact. Political and cultural correctness tipped from being a vague concept to non-existence. Differences were considered fair game for scorn.

"Nobody paid any more attention to me than they did to the bat bag," said Meyers about his start in the minor leagues.

When a spitball pitcher in Harrisburg purposely switched up his signals, causing five passed balls in two innings, Meyers rebelled.

"That did me more good than anything that ever happened to me," he said. "It made me mad. I had been timid and now I was mad enough to be brave."

Meyers, remember, had attended Dartmouth.

"This is a strange country to me," he once said. "I'm a stranger in a strange land."

For the scattering of Native Americans who played baseball in the first quarter of the 20th century, first names were often substituted with the same generic nickname – Chief Meyers, Chief Bender, Chief Chouneau, Chief Johnson, Chief Yellowhorse, Chief Youngblood . . . Jim Thorpe, Zack Wheat, and a few others somehow managed to escape the brand.

Of course, the "Indian Wars" were not that far back in history, the Wounded Knee Massacre having occurred in December 1890. There still remained much bitterness and misunderstanding.

"The wicked do not live out half their days," said Bucknell President John Howard Harris in 1898. "Non-moralized people do not live to a great age. The North American Indians die on an average in their 20th year. The whites of Washington City, for instance, live for an average of 50 years. That is about the average of people as nearly Christianized as Americans."

That was one of the few teachings from his old pastor that Matty never accepted, chalking it up to the blather of an older generation.

Matty was quite close with Meyers, Thorpe, and Philadelphia's Bender. He usually called Meyers by his first name, Jack, and, like Connie Mack, called Bender by his middle name, Albert. While the fans remained brutal, Bender never backed down, referring to them as "foreigners."

Still, as much as Native Americans were taunted, at least they could play. African Americans were not even allowed in the ballpark.

Racial lines were unbendable. On a trip to Cuba in 1911, Matty pitched against Jose Mendez, known locally as "The Black Mathewson." Although Big Six and the Giants earned a 3-0 shutout, Mendez was spectacular.

"If the unwritten law of baseball didn't ban Negroes from the Major Leagues," said McGraw, "I would give $50,000 for him and think I was getting a bargain."

Of course, Muggsy knew the youngster would never pass the rigid major-league color barrier.

Christy would have welcomed the diversity. But, like most white Americans at the time, both he and Jane quietly accepted the status quo.

While nicknames could be humorous or fanciful, they also could demean. Luther "Dummy" Taylor was New York's third ace, winning 115 games in nine seasons. He played in the majors at the same time as Dummy Hoy, Dummy Dundon, Dummy Deegan, Dummy Leitner, Dummy Lynch, Dummy Murphy and Dummy Stephenson . . . all deaf mutes.

Without doubt, verbal ammunition could be insensitive, vicious.

Although McGraw may have designed a roughhouse roster – and despite the regular measure of ethnic slurs, taunts, and insults that he and his players heaved at the opposition – the manager made certain that scorn and prejudice did not creep into his dugout. Under McGraw's iron watch, every player was embraced within the Giants' family.

"We could all read and speak sign language," said outfielder Fred Snodgrass, "because Dummy Taylor took it as an affront if you didn't learn to converse with him. If we went to the vaudeville show, he wanted to know what the joke was, and somebody had to tell him. So we all learned. We practiced all the time."

CHAPTER THIRTEEN

Summer 1911 . . . West Point, New York

Christy was standing on the Army infield, relieved that McGraw had not asked him to work today. The real season was barely half over and he wanted to conserve his energy for the next series in Boston. But, here they were for an exhibition game at the Military Academy, so the least he could do was sign some autographs before the players took the field.

"Mr. Mathewson, Sir," asked one of the cadets, "just how perfect is your control?"

"Well, Johnny Evers of the Cubs says I can find the inside of a tin can from the pitcher's box," Matty replied. "I've never tried that, but I suppose he's right."

By now about a dozen young cadets had joined the conversation.

"How many times could you do that?" asked another.

"Well, to my mind, I think I could do it every time."

The group seemed amazed, but one cadet was not so sure.

"Mr. Mathewson, don't get me wrong, Sir, I think you're a great pitcher," he said, "but I don't think anyone can be perfect."

"You're right," said Matty with a smile, "but a good pitcher needs a healthy ego."

"Sir, would you be interested in a wager that you couldn't hit the same spot, say 20 times in a row?" the cadet slyly wondered.

Matty considered the challenge. A bet?

"Hmmm, can I use my catcher?"

"Yes sir," said another cadet.

Matty turned to find Chief Meyers, standing near home plate.

"Hey Jack, how about catching some pitches?" he yelled, producing a $20 bill for the cadets.

"Same spot 20 times," said Matty.

"Your catcher can't move his glove."

"No problem," said Big Six. "What kind of odds are you willing to give me?"

The cadets huddled, excitedly discussing a plan.

"How about 12-1 odds, Sir?"

"That would be $240," said Matty. "You boys have that much money to lose?"

They laughed.

"We each have $20, Sir."

"Good," said Matty, moving to the rubber.

"Jack, don't move your glove."

"I never do," the catcher replied, figuring the cadets were toast.

Big Six then threw 20 straight strikes, Meyers never even twitching. Without saying a word, Matty turned to his stunned audience and collected $240.

"Thank you men," he said as he walked toward home plate to split the profit with his catcher and partner in crime.

Although the years began to pile, The Christian Gentleman was remarkably consistent, compiling records of 26-13 in 1911, followed by 23-12 and 25-11, always keeping his earned run average at 2.00 or under. In 1913, the veteran hurler would win the ERA title for the fifth time. Four seasons, he had led the NL in victories, five in strikeouts.

Simply told, he had great control. During the 1913 campaign, he threw 68 straight innings without allowing a base on balls, finishing the season with only 21 walks in 306 innings.

"But they aint nobody in the world," wrote Ring Lardner, "can stick a ball as near as where they want to stick it as he can."

Following that second-place finish in 1910, the Giants ran off three straight pennants. Matty was steady.

"After he had used up his early supply of youthful vigor, he remained a great pitcher for years by pitching with his mind," said Jane. "His brain had card-indexed all the pitches he had thrown to various batters and his mathematical mind had figured out the percentage of a batter hitting every kind of pitch he had at his command."

Max Carey, the Pirates great centerfielder, was also a huge fan: "I've watched Mathewson closely and I've never seen him pitch a ballgame in which he didn't look as if he were having a lot of fun. It doesn't look to be work to him, but only pure sport, an afternoon romp."

But it wasn't all fun. From 1911-13, the Giants would lose three World Series in a row – twice to the Athletics and once to the Red Sox.

Perhaps the 1912 World Series against Boston was the toughest. In extra innings of the seventh and deciding game, the Giants had taken a 2-1 lead with the Red Sox batting in the bottom of the 10th. The Great Mathewson was cruising, the sellout crowd in the newly constructed Fenway Park near quiet with the certainty their beloved Sox would fall. And, when leadoff batter Clyde Engle hit a routine fly ball to center, there was a momentary moan that somehow turned to a mind-boggling roar . . . Giants' outfielder Fred Snodgrass had dropped the ball. Inexplicably, it fell right out of his glove. No outs, tying run on second.

What is lost in most history books is that Harry Hooper lined Matty's next pitch to deep right center for what looked to be certain extra bases. But, on a desperate sprint, Snodgrass made a miracle catch for the first out. After Steve Yerkes was intentionally walked, it seemed as if the Giants might be out of the woods as Tris Speaker hit a high pop foul between home and first. Fred Merkle had the beat, but Matty called for his catcher to make the grab. Merkle stopped, Chief Meyers dove, the ball skipped off his glove.

"Well, you just called the wrong man," Speaker yelled at Matty. "It's gonna cost you this ball game."

It did. Speaker singled Engle home with the tying run, Yerkes finding third. Larry Garner followed with a long sacrifice fly to right and Engle easily scored as Fenway shook with hysteria.

Boston 3, New York 2 . . . the Red Sox were world champs.

Matty stood stunned on the mound, then slowly walked to the dugout, his eyes staring at the ground.

The euphoria of victory did not blind the Boston fans of their sympathy for the losing pitcher. In the October 17, 1912 issue of the *Boston Globe*, T.H. Murnane wrote:

> "Mathewson, the baseball genius, was heartbroken and tears rolled down his sunburned cheeks as he was consoled by his fellow players. The greatest pitcher of all time had lost, after pitching a remarkable game. It was not fault of his."

The press refused to blame "the old master" for any of the Giants' mishaps during the three-year postseason tank, instead charging that his teammates "were like pebbles on a barren shore."

"I wouldn't have minded it half so much if it had been any pitcher but Matty," said Jack "Chief" Meyers. "I will regret to my dying day that this grand fellow was forced to suffer for our sins."

Christy and his catcher, Jack "Chief" Meyers.

A year later, Matty wrote "Why We Lost Three World's Championships" for *Everybody's Magazine*.

According to Christy, because John McGraw "absolutely directs the game," most of his players "cannot stand on their own feet because they have never had to."

Matty further charged that the "Giants are the greatest newspaper ballclub I know. Most of the men read everything that is printed about them."

Put these facts together and the team developed, for three straight Octobers, a bad case of World Series nerves.

"The Giants did not obey orders," wrote Christy. "They either forgot or else convinced themselves that they knew more than the wonderful little manager who had guided them so long. Not only did they fail to execute McGraw's commands properly, but they became so upset that they made bullheaded plays that you would never have seen during the regular league campaign."

Amazingly, Christy Mathewson was somehow able to be critical without causing waves.

"I sincerely hope no one will accuse me of poor sportsmanship," Matty concluded. "I have not squealed, only analyzed the situation from things that I know."

On the baseball diamond, Christopher Mathewson relished the limelight. He loved the big crowds.

"The air is bristling with excitement when a partisan throng fills the stands," he wrote in *Pearson's Magazine*, "and the players are jammed with ginger."

He also reiterated that McGraw was a master at manipulating the rooters . . . "a clever man and good actor."

Christy, that once shy college kid, had matured into a charismatic showman, entering the stadium wearing a long linen auto driver duster over his uniform. After the 1912 World Series loss to the Red Sox, Giants' fans had given him a 40 horsepower Columbia Touring automobile that cost $5,000. His grand pregame entrances were simply a way to thank his devoted admirers.

Big Six was "king, emperor and ruler of all baseball," the press acknowledged.

He definitely enjoyed driving that big, magnificent Columbia. While he was usually quite conscious of the many kids gleefully running beside his car, he was once fined $100 for driving 31 miles an hour in a 10 mph zone.

Jane was actually one of the first female motorists in New York City. Most of the women who could afford to own a car had the wealth to hire a chauffer. And they didn't necessarily want to deal with the cumbersome hand cranks to start the engine.

That didn't faze Jane, who drove as much for sport as convenience. Unfortunately, Jane would also get nailed with a speeding ticket, breaking the law at 11 miles an hour.

Truthfully, the Mathewsons didn't need a car for driving around town, their apartment overlooking the Polo Grounds. Except for the days the team was out of town, Christy worked in the afternoon and was always home before evening. In fact, Jane could see the stadium scoreboard from the kitchen window.

"As soon as the game reached the seventh inning," she told the *Literary Digest,* "I knew it was time to put on my potatoes."

Jane only attended the games that her husband was scheduled to pitch. She was not alone.

"Fans not only called up the club asking when Matty would pitch," she said, "but called up our apartment as well."

She was happy to answer their questions. The *Literary Digest* described Jane as "intelligent and quite beautiful."

There is no doubt that the heart of Jane and Christy Mathewson's life was their son. Christy joked that the first thing he would always see before entering their top floor apartment at 155th Avenue and St. Nicholas Place was Sonny's nose pressed against the windowpane.

Jane often wondered who was the biggest kid?

"He would come home grinning," Jane recalled of her husband, "like a boy who had committed some impish deed, and say, 'Well, I took those Reds again today.'"

CHAPTER THIRTEEN

There was a rule in the Mathewson household, apparently initiated by Jane, that discussions about the day's game not be carried to the dinner table. All things considered, they were simply a normal family.

As Sonny began to see the world beyond Washington Heights, he loved the many trips to see the relatives in Factoryville and Lewisburg, always a magnificent taste of his parent's small town country upbringing. Still, Sonny and his puppy, Polo Grounds, had their own land of wonder with a full run of Coogan's Bluff and beyond. Growing quickly, the boy was smart, curious, and did exceptionally well in school, where he had a ton of friends. On Sundays, he attended church with one or both parents, depending on the baseball schedule.

Always a welcome guest in the Giants' clubhouse, Sonny would be greeted by a parade of amazing ballplayers, instant playmates ever on their best behavior. Unfortunately, the first time that the youngster visited the dugout, he accidentally dropped a bat on his dad's toe.

Big for his age and quite athletic, Sonny often played catch with a father who never pushed, just encouraged. He also had his own set of miniature golf clubs, the three Mathewsons often playing at the Pelham and Van Courtlandt courses.

A newspaper headline in 1912 introduced six-year-old Sonny as "America's Proudest Boy."

The youngster was never consumed with fame; his upbringing too grounded, his interests too diverse. Eventually, of course, he realized that his father was the most idolized man in America.

During a quick train stop on the way to Chicago, Matty was playing bridge with McGraw and two teammates. A man jumped on the train, introducing himself as a schoolmaster who had brought 40 boys to the station in hopes of seeing Matty. There was a time in his life that Matty would have cringed at the request, perhaps even made an excuse. Instead, he walked onto the station platform and shook hands with each boy. Big Six then "stood in the doorway of his Pullman and waved to them as the train pulled out of the station."

More and more, he appreciated the significance of being a role model for youth. In 1915, speaking to 550 boys at the New York Juvenile Asylum at Dobbs Ferry, Matty asked them to consider a clean and upright character.

"I might lecture you boys about control being the big thing in life," said Christy, "but just now I'll talk about pitching, and in that, also, control is everything."

When it came to self-control, Christy Jr. emulated his parents. He also enjoyed music and loved to read, particularly when he could curl up in dad's chair.

In 1914, when Lewis Theiss published his first adventure book, *In Camp at Fort Brady,* he presented a copy to Sonny, who became an instant fan. Matty's old friend and fraternity brother would eventually write 42 youth books, many focusing on aviation. While the Giants were heroes who Sonny could see and touch at any time, it was the great aviators – the Wright Brothers, Glenn Curtiss, Harriet Quimby – who soared through the youngster's imagination.

The New York Giants could have fielded a powerful football team . . . Mathewson, Meyers, Merkle, Moose McCormick . . . Jim Thorpe.

The year after he won two gold medals at the 1912 Summer Olympics, the celebrated Thorpe joined the Giants. Considered the most versatile athlete in the world, Thorpe had starred in track and field, baseball, football, basketball, and lacrosse at Carlisle. In 1911, he was even the intercollegiate ballroom dancing champion. That was the same year he had kicked four field goals and scored a touchdown as Carlisle upset Harvard.

But, stepping into professional baseball would certainly be a stretch for Thorpe. An amazing athlete, yes . . . ability to hit the curve, no.

Still, at the 1913 spring training camp in Marlin, Texas, the press crowned Thorpe the center of attention. McGraw was not thrilled with the hype or the rookie, although Christy was quite considerate, saying that Thorpe had "athletic instinct" and would hit .300 within a year.

Thorpe would only play 19 games that season and bat 35 times, a meager .143 batting average. Thorpe would describe the Giants as a "wildest, fighting, and blood thirsty bunch he'd ever known."

And that's from the guy who, during the baseball offseason, played professional football for the Canton Bulldogs. Eight years younger than Big Six, Thorpe would kid Matty that he would get him a tryout with

Canton . . . if the Bulldogs didn't already have the greatest running back and kicker of all-time.

Mathewson and Thorpe would share star billing on the famous Baseball World Tour during the offseason of 1913-14. Starting in Cincinnati, the Giants and White Sox began a thunderous 30,000-mile adventure through 27 American cities and 13 foreign countries, the intent to bring the game of baseball to the rest of the world. The two teams had played 30 games in 33 days when they hit San Francisco on November 15. After pitching the Giants to a 6-3 victory before a sellout crowd of 10,000 fans at Exhibition Park, Matty held seven-year-old Sonny in his arms and announced that his family would be staying on the West Coast for the rest of the winter. Ever susceptible to seasickness, he was not ready for the long journey across the seven seas. It proved to be a wise decision since the voyage to Japan would be hammered by a surprise typhoon with 60-foot waves.

They tour would shine from Australia to Hong Kong, the capitals of Europe to Cairo. But Matty's arm needed a rest, the three Mathewsons settling in Southern California.

Los Angeles had more than quadrupled since the turn of the century, now busting with more than 400,000 residents. From the San Gabriel Mountains to the Pacific Ocean, the beautiful valley included endless miles of orange groves, mild winter weather, and pure air. It was a paradise where Matty could play golf and, hopefully, not be recognized. They rented a comfortable home at 1337 West 47th Street, Sonny enrolling in elementary school.

On January 8, 1914, a man from Chicago sent a postcard to New York. He addressed it to "6" . . . nothing more, just a large, four-inch long numerical six, cut from a newspaper headline and pasted on the card. On the back he had written, "Matty, if you get this please let me know. G. Irwin." With a two-cent stamp, it headed to Gotham, where the postal clerk immediately realized the recipient was Big Six. With a blue pencil, he wrote in the corner of the card next to the stamp and below the giant "6" to "Try Los Angeles, Cal." The postcard was forwarded across the country, the clerk in L.A. handing it to a mail carrier who delivered it directly to Matty . . . so much for keeping a low profile.

Jane would keep that card as one of her prize possessions.

Entering 1914, Matty felt his first twinge of age discrimination, a few suddenly noisy skeptics wondering if the tank still had any gas. He was 33 years old, his arm had weathered more than 4,200 innings in 14 major-league seasons, and nobody pitches forever. Ring Lardner blazed to his good friend's defense:

> "Leave him get warmed up, then give him a good look. This spring was hard on old soupers. You can't expect a bird that's been hurlin' the pill in the big show all these years to set the league afire. Don't talk like he was gone and ask me what kind of a pitcher he *was*."

Thank you, Mr. Lardner. Matty would go 24-13 in 1914, completing 29 of 35 starts, and walking only 23 batters in 312 innings. However, the Giants finished second to the surprising Boston Braves, a great disappointment for those New Yorkers seeking revenge after three straight postseason stumbles.

"The mighty Mathewson was generally carrying a whole ball club on his back," wrote Damon Runyon. "Time and time again it fell to him to fight the crucial battles . . . and he rarely failed."

Runyon surmised that although Matty could not pitch forever, "in sagacity, in sheer mastery of his craft, he is probably still the greatest of them all."

Runyon was simply confirming public opinion. The gifted veteran had been sailing along as if he could win 20 games a year for another 20 seasons. Well, he had won 20-or-more for 12 straight years, including four with more than 30 victories. In fact, his lowest total over that span had been 22 wins in 1906, the year he had diphtheria.

CHAPTER FOURTEEN

October 1914 . . . New York

The three Mathewsons and their dog, Polo Grounds, were walking through Central Park, a perfect Sunday in late October. The picturesque landscape was alive with trees, beautifully painted leaves in shades of red, orange, and yellow. The path was also crowded with people, an uncommonly warm spurt of weather having energized the entire city.

Christy and Jane had been discussing the statistical probability of walking for three minutes without being stopped by an autograph seeker. Numbed to his father's celebrity status, eight-year-old Sonny was more interested in his pup's sudden interest in a pretty Golden Lab.

"I think once we hit a hundred autographs, we should just start running," laughed Jane.

"Perhaps if I dropped my hat low over my face," said Christy, or, better yet, grew a beard for the offseason."

"A wonderful idea," quipped Jane.

There now seemed to be a good trail without many people, except for an approaching man, quite tall and thin. The stranger walked past, tipping his hat to Jane.

Christy gulped . . . the man was cross-eyed.

Quickly, Big Six grabbed his new hat from the top of his head and spit in it.

Sonny, spit in your hat," Christy whispered, rather frantic.

Without hesitation, the boy did as he was told, pulling down his hat and inducing a strong spit.

"A cross-eyed man?" asked Sonny.

"Yes," answered Christy, still unnerved. "Jane, spit in your hat."

"I will not," she answered. "You boys can play your little games of jinxes, but I am a lady."

"Doesn't matter," said Christy, "spit in your hat . . . hurry."

With a smirk on her face, Jane unfastened her pretty hat and blew a fake air of spit into it."

"Good enough," said one of baseball's most intelligent players, "we're safe."

"And women don't have the right to vote," Jane muttered under her breath.

Chapter Eleven of Christy's book, *Pitching in a Pinch*, was dedicated to "Jinxes and What They Mean to a Ball-Player."

Aside from the "cross-eyed man" curse – a fear held by every respectable ballplayer of the time – Matty would never warm up with a third baseman . . . bad luck.

"Ballplayers are among the most superstitious persons in the world," wrote Matty. "A really true, on-the-level, honest-to-jiminy jinx can do all sorts of mean things."

New York's great infielder, Art Devlin, would crumble if anyone in the dugout hummed or sang, declaring war if a teammate sat in his lucky spot on the bench.

Mired in an unlucky pitching drought, Red Ames of the Giants started wearing a lucky multi-colored necktie under his uniform. He had the ability, Matty pointed out, the jinx-busting scarf now giving him confidence.

"Ames used to sleep with it under his pillow alongside of his bank roll," said Matty, "and he didn't lose another game until the very end of the season."

John McGraw would personally terminate his team's batting slumps by bringing a load of empty barrels to the park.

"That is why I maintain he is the greatest manager of them all," said Big Six. "He takes advantage of the little things, even the superstitions."

While the Giants freaked if one bat became crossed with another, the Athletics created a ritual of throwing their bats wildly into the air in front of their dugout whenever they needed to turn the tide of a game.

Baseball superstition can get complicated.

"I have seen a ball club," wrote Matty, "composed of educated men, carry a Kansas farmer, with two or three screws ratting loose in his dome, around the circuit because he came as a prophet and said that he was accompanied by Miss Fickle Fortune."

That ball club, of course, would be the Giants. In 1911, it was the presence of Charlie Faust, a rather strange character who had a vision that he would lead the Giants to a world championship. Whenever he talked his way into the dugout, the Giants won. Of course, the days he was missing – usually performing vaudeville – the Giants would lose. McGraw thought Charley was a quack, but the players loved his humor and you don't mess with the supernatural.

But, alas, at the 1911 World Series, the Athletics conjured a magical antidote.

"They have a combination bat boy and mascot who is a hunchback," said Matty, "and he out-jinxed our champion jinx killer."

The Athletics even voted their mascot a share of the World Series earnings. Poor Charley Faust had to return to vaudeville.

Population in the United States passed 100 million people in 1915, but the two big leagues had suffered a one-third loss in attendance the previous year. That was the fault of the new Federal League, which stole many of the top players with the lure of higher salaries. The Federals heavily courted Christy, the Brooklyn franchise "willing to pay Big Six any amount of money." Christy, however, was content with his $12,000 salary.

"I will not use the offer to get more money from the Giants," he said. "I will not pit the clubs against each other."

If there was excitement in Brooklyn, it was a dream.

"I never had the slightest idea of accepting their offers," Matty said.

Matty also had quiet concerns for the new league's viability. His instincts were correct. The Federal League would fold after two seasons.

The Giants visit Havana.

While rumors about Matty switching leagues were swirling, he and Jane were on another winter trip to Cuba with many of the Giants players and wives. Part of John McGraw's travel agenda was a mule race, one more chance for the old coacher to best his prize pupil. Naturally, Matty was certain he could pick the faster mule.

Blanche McGraw vividly recalled the wild stretch run:

> "With the finish only a few yards away, Christy's mule was far ahead but happened to see an open gate that led to the stables. The mule stopped . . . he wanted no more racing. While he stood there, John's mule thundered across the finish line.
>
> 'Don't ever bet on mules, Mr. Mathewson,' John cautioned and held out his hand for payment. 'They're not reliable.'"

At least Matty did better at the American club in Havana, sweeping the top Cuban players at checkers and cards.

Entering the 1915 season, Matty's control was flawless, his mind in total control . . . but his shoulder and back would suffer major problems. Almost overnight, it seemed, his body weathered. His 3.58 ERA was the worst since his three-game rookie struggle in 1900. His won-lost mark plunged to 8-14, the first time in a dozen years he had not been a 20-game winner. Just as strange, the Giants finished dead last.

"I'm going to devote the off-season to trying to tame the pain that still lurks in my neck and is jumping out of the left shoulder," said Matty, who still found time for trap shooting.

Christy and three other major-league stars – Chief Bender, Otis Crandall, and Harry Davis – embarked on an 18-city tour that included western stops in Omaha, Des Moines, and Minneapolis. With each participant shooting 100 targets, the four players opposed a team of the area's top amateurs and "awakened a great enthusiasm for the sport." Naturally, the ballplayers kept statistics, Bender ultimately crowned "King of the Traps." At Syracuse, the future Hall of Fame pitcher hit 99 of 100 targets, a low of 83 at Toledo. Christy, who had never shot indoors and was still injured, would finish third overall, a low of 50 at Cincinnati and a personal best 89 at Chicago.

In November 1915, Matty considered an offer to manage the Harvard baseball team.

"Harvard has been left open for me," he said, "but I hope I am back in the old uniform and ready to deliver. I would hate to think I had taken it off for the last time."

The dominance was gone, but the adoration from fans and peers never wavered. The relationship was simply too deep.

"I was a rough kid," said Babe Ruth, the young pitching sensation of the Boston Red Sox. "Maybe I didn't always know my lessons, but I always knew how many games Matty had won and lost. I read everything about him that I could get my hands on."

Hoping he had recovered, Matty had a strong start in 1916 with four complete games and a shutout against the Boston Braves. As his 2.33 ERA might attest, even an aging Mathewson was better than most pitchers in baseball. But the back began hurting once again and the shoulder was still sore, McGraw unceremoniously pulling him from the starting rotation. Matty had a 3-4 record in mid-July when he sat down with his manager for a long chat.

McGraw knew Big Six wanted to manage and understood his preference would be New York. But, at 43 years old, Muggsy was nowhere near retirement. What if he could work a deal with another club? Matty agreed.

On July 20, 1916, the Giants and Cincinnati Reds pulled off a shocking trade. New York received Buck Herzog and Red Killefer; Cincy got Bill McKechnie, Edd Roush, and Christy Mathewson.

Big Six would be a player/manager of a team *Sport Magazine* described as a "dull and monotonous plateau of slight accomplishment." Still, he was excited for the challenge. Owner August Hermann, known for his fairness, maintained Christy's $12,000 a year salary while also giving the rookie manager control of player acquisitions.

Looking back, the Reds clearly got the best of the deal with New York. Roush, a 23-year-old centerfielder with great potential, had seen sporadic action with the Giants. In Cincinnati, he would become an instant superstar.

However, the monster story of that mid-summer day was the unbelievable melancholy ripping through the heart of the baseball world. After 17 seasons with the Giants, the greatest hurler in history was changing uniforms to become a player/manager. To many, it was beyond belief.

"It wasn't easy for me to part with Matty," said John McGraw. "He not only was the greatest pitcher I ever saw, but he is my friend."

"Of course, I realize I'm through as a pitcher," said Big Six. "But I appreciate McGraw making a place for me in baseball and getting me this managing job. He's doing me a favor, and I thanked him for it."

In his managerial debut at Cincinnati's Redland Field, Matty brought home a winner as young Roush led the Reds to a 6-4 win over the Phillies.

One of Matty's first decisions was to hire a team trainer, his old Bucknell football coach, George "Doc" Hoskins.

Christopher Mathewson would pitch one final game. As part of a Labor Day extravaganza in Chicago, the Reds and Cubs agreed to revive the old pitching matchup of Matty against Mordecai "Three Finger"

Brown. A huge poster appeared throughout the Windy City, featuring a picture of the two legendary rivals under the headline: "Brown versus Mathewson – Greatest Treat of the Year for Baseball Fans." Both men vowed they would go the distance.

The veteran rivals had met 25 times, Brown winning 13 and Matty 11. The most important encounter was the infamous 1908 playoff game, won by the Cubs. With 611 victories between them – plus another five each in the World Series – this would close both of their brilliant careers. That Matty and Brownie had both lost their dominance hardly mattered to the sellout crowd at Chicago's Weeghman Park.

It was a wild game with Brown getting roughed up for 19 hits and Matty 15. As if they were now better batsmen than pitchers, Matty had three hits (including a double) and Brownie two. What hurt Mathewson the most was that Laughing Larry Doyle now played second base for the Cubs, blistering his old buddy for a double and two singles. However, with a 10-8 Cincy win, Christy Mathewson notched his final victory . . . career number 373 . . . the only time he had ever pitched in the majors for a team other than the Giants.

Matty made a graceful transition.

"How I love the game, the fighting, the glamour and the good will of the public," he said. "I don't know how I shall get along without them."

The Reds were 25-43 under Matty's watch, finishing in a last-place tie with the Cardinals, the title won by the Brooklyn Robins, the franchise that had already been the Bridegrooms, Superbas, and Trolley Dodgers. Would they ever decide on a name?

Despite the 1916 results, there was optimism in Cincinnati. Hal Chase had won the NL batting crown and Roush was easily the best young ball-player in the game. Matty also felt he could mold a good group of young pitchers to complement the talents of veteran' Fred Toney.

Christy also picked up an old friend, Jim Thorpe, on a loan from the Giants. In three seasons, Thorpe had a meager .195 batting average with New York, but still showed potential. The press predicted that Big Six would "accelerate Jim Thorpe's development as a big leaguer."

They were right.

Thorpe had a solid year, as did the Reds, jumping from last to fourth in 1917, a winning season before a franchise-record 270,000 fans. Many came to see Roush, who hit a sparkling .341, and Prince Hal Chase, a glorious first baseman who had led the league in hitting the previous season. And Thorpe was also a big feature until the Giants grabbed him back late in the season. Of course, another reason the fans packed Redland Field was to catch a glimpse of the legendary Big Six.

Behind the curtain, however, there was turmoil. Matty was beginning to suspect Chase of throwing games. The manager watched, calculated, and boiled.

There also was the backdrop of world war, the United States having declared war on Germany five days before the 1917 baseball season began. Big Six immediately took a leading role in selling war bonds.

At the same time, Matty's thoughts were acutely drawn to Factoryville. His brother Henry, now 31 years old, was fighting the final stages of tuberculosis. He died the first day of July, leaving a wife and four children. Christy, Jane, and Sonny took the first train home. The national obituaries would remember Henry as the ill-fated brother who pitched three games in the majors, going 0-1 with the record 14 walks in one game. To Christy, of course, the stats were frivolous . . . he had lost his last brother.

Roush and the Reds were even better in 1918, a season with a few more twists. In early August, rookie pitcher Jimmy Ring entered a tight ballgame, Chase approaching the mound from his first-base position.

"I've got some money going on this game, kid." Chase whispered. "There's something in it for you if you lose."

Although Ring tried to ignore the bribe and win the game, the Reds would fall. Afterwards, $50 appeared in Ring's locker. He reported the incident to his manager.

On August 9, Mathewson suspended Chase for "indifferent play" and forwarded his list of reasons to NL president John Heydler. It would take months for the league to hear all sides of the story and make a final decision.

Meanwhile, the revitalized Reds would finish in third place behind the Giants and champion' Cubs, who would lose the Fall Classic to Ruth and the Red Sox.

But final standings and World Series showdowns were insignificant to the reach of World War I. The United States had now been at war for more than a year with 10,000 Americans leaving each day to fight in Europe.

Christy privately talked with Jane about joining the fight. She stressed his value on the home front. Although, at 38, he was too old to be drafted, Matty nevertheless felt a duty to enlist, particularly in light of the 254 other big-league ballplayers going to war. On August 27, with less than a week remaining in the regular season, Christy would manage his final game. He had accepted a commission as Captain in the Chemical Warfare Service of the U.S. Army.

Christy Jr. was excited that his father was joining the fight. Young Christy was especially interested in the air war, having crowned his own hero in Captain Eddie Rickenbacker, the former racecar driver. He cheered when Manfred von Richthofen – the Red Baron – was killed in April; nearly cried when Lt. Quentin Roosevelt was shot down near Chamery, France in July. Quentin, the youngest son of former President Teddy Roosevelt, was flying with the 95th "Kicking Mule" Aero Squadron when he died on Bastille Day (July 14). He was only 20 years old. Christy Jr. was not yet 12, but he was definitely growing up fast.

It would not be the war effort that Captain Mathewson intended to fight. In September, he became horribly seasick crossing the Atlantic. Barely recovered, he was hospitalized in Chaumont with influenza, an epidemic sweeping the world. When he finally joined the Gas and Flame Division, he was reunited with his old baseball buddy, Ty Cobb. The irascible Cobb never hid his admiration for Matty.

"You couldn't help but love Matty," said the Georgia Peach.

While Germany was close to surrender, Matty accidentally caught a heavy dose of poison gas during training.

"Ty, when we were in there, I got a good dose of the stuff," he told Cobb. "I feel terrible."

"I saw Christy Mathewson doomed to die," Cobb would later say.

After the war ended in November 1918, Christy was assigned to Flanders, where he was exposed to another dose of mustard gas while examining ammunition dumps. His lungs were wracked.

He sent Jane a host of postcards, many picturing French soldiers marching into Metz. Christy was stunned that the French thought baseball was "brutal."

Meanwhile, back at the National League office in New York, the rather substantial evidence in the Hal Chase bribery case was thoroughly reviewed. Even John McGraw testified that one of his Giants was approached by Chase to throw a game. Although President Heydler privately believed that Chase was guilty, he ruled that there was "insufficient evidence" should Chase appeal the matter in a court of law, mainly because Matty was overseas and unable to testify.

Matty was also in the hospital, battling a second round of the flu when August Hermann sent cablegrams asking him to again manage the Reds. Matty never received them and Hermann was forced to hire a new manager, Pat Moran.

Jane was deeply worried when Christy returned from Europe on the Steamship Rotterdam. His skin was pale and pasty; his gait was slow, his body excessively fatigued . . . and he had a deep cough that would not subside. The doctors diagnosed it as chronic bronchitis . . . he just needed rest and warmth.

In the spring of 1919, John McGraw signed Christy to a $5,000 contract as the Giants' pitching coach.

"It is my purpose to groom Matty for the job as manager," said McGraw, "and turn the team over to him in two or three years so that I can retire."

Matty had accumulated a managing mark of 164-176 with the Reds, but he had done a great job of building a contender.

"If Mathewson had any fault as a manager," wrote the *New York Times*, "it was that he was too gentle in dealing with the players. He was an easy going leader."

Joining the Giants at their Florida spring training site in Gainesville, Matty was reunited with Larry Doyle, Art Fletcher, Jim Thorpe, and Fred Toney. In New York, Jane could once again see Blanche on a daily basis and Christy Jr. – now 13 and officially graduated to be called "Son" by his parents – was thrilled to be back at the Polo Grounds. It all seemed a natural fit for Matty, except for two irritating problems. Playing first base for New York was none other than Prince Hal Chase. They would not speak to one another for the entire season. Also, Matty became more and more frustrated that he had not recovered his strength.

Nevertheless, Big Six molded a solid staff with great control, even coaching Jesse Barnes, a previously journeyman hurler, to a league best 25-9 record. Nevertheless, the Giants finished second to Cincinnati. That was the year of the infamous Black Sox scandal, the Reds winning the world title as the heavily favored Chicago White Sox tumbled rather suspiciously. Working as a correspondent for the *New York Evening World*, Matty saw the fix unfold from the press box, comparing observations with sportswriter Hugh Fullerton of the *Chicago Herald*. They would send their notes to the National Baseball Commission. Eventually, eight White Sox players would be forever banned from the game.

Christy was back with the Giants in 1920, his nemesis Hal Chase having been released after further evidence surfaced that he indeed was fixing games. No other major league team would sign Prince Hal, even though he was still one of the finest fielders and hitters in the game.

As the season started, it became painfully obvious that Matty could not shake his health problems. He was frail and ashen, battled a constant low-grade fever, and his appetite had vanished. Returning to the doctor, he received a new and dreadful diagnosis. Matty had an advanced case of tuberculosis. He was given six months to live.

Matty left the Giants, traveling north with the family and dog to Saranac, New York, home of the Trudeau Sanitarium, one of the most notable tuberculosis treatment and research centers in the world.

Back in 1884, when Dr. Edward Livingston Trudeau founded his "wilderness cure" sanitarium at Saranac Lake, one in seven Americans died of tuberculosis. Starting with a cottage and several beds, Trudeau believed that the altitude of the Adirondack Mountains was restorative, that the "White Plague" could be fought with "fresh air, rest, restrained exercise, and good food."

There was great progress and guarded hope. By 1920, tuberculosis was still killing more than 100,000 Americans each year, but had steadily been declining to almost half the death rate of the early 1900s.

When the Mathewson family arrived in July 1920 – five years after Dr. Trudeau's death – the center had expanded to 150 cottages with nearly 2,000 patients, a landscape of exquisitely manicured gardens fronting woods, lakes, streams, and mountains.

Christy hardly noticed the beauty . . .

CHAPTER FIFTEEN

Late Fall 1920 . . . Saranac Lake

The room was dark, the day gone. Christy realized he was once again awake . . . the painful cough and uncontrollable chills, shallow breaths prodding raw cavities in his lungs, his body unable to work . . . so terribly tired.

Christy's mind twitched, as if urgently lost within a dream . . . searching to remember the feeling of strength . . . deep breaths and tight muscles . . . to run from the dugout, to throw a fastball on the outside corner, to dropkick a football without pain . . . days that were now nothing more than a remote shadow.

In a comfortable cottage at Saranac Lake, Jane dedicated her every moment to nursing her husband in his battle against the "White Plague." Now 14, Christy Jr. followed his mother's every instruction, assisting as best he could. It didn't help when he fell out of a tree and broke his arm, but that would pale to his father's grave condition.

After a dangerous and excruciating surgery, Matty remained bedridden, unable to even sit up. Newspapers around the nation were reporting that he was near death . . . and this was true.

But in February of 1921, he was starting to feel just a bit better, even able to sit up in bed for short segments. With the help of Jane and Son, he began moving around the apartment in a wheel chair, then playing chess and checkers, looking out the window at Mount Pisgah, studying natural history.

Harry Hoffer, the one-time running champion who also was battling the disease, would bring Christy the daily newspapers from the railroad depot.

His reading appetite was stronger – Rudyard Kipling's *The Years Between*, William Roscoe Thayer's *Theodore Roosevelt*, and Irving Bacheller's *A Man for the Ages*. Christy Jr. even loaned his father *The Hidden Aerial* by Lewis Theiss.

When they couldn't visit, John and Blanche telephoned. Christy was still weak, but soon he was starting to take short walks and automobile rides, Jane driving. He even conducted a few brief interviews with some of the reporters that he considered more as friends.

"The doctors say he has a chance," wrote Bozeman Bolger. "That's why I know that he will win."

For the public, Christy downplayed the affliction.

"Get out of your head that I am a real invalid or in any kind of bad shape," said Christy. "I don't know how the news of my illness got out. It sure spread. Somebody blabbed. I was surprised to find that some of the press reports have me at death's door."

Christy blamed the tuberculosis on a bronchial cold that infected his throat and right lung.

"When McGraw found out about it he insisted upon my being shipped to the Adirondacks, so here I am. Take a peek at those hills; look at this beautiful lake."

Of course, he knew how sick he had been, how he was far from cured. But he would fight, he would recover . . . just like *Pitching In A Pinch* . . . a regular Frank Merriwell . . . he'd somehow survive this scrape.

The stories caught the nation's passion, Christy hurling baseball analogies to define his battle for life:

"You will never win if you quit."

"The game is never over until the last inning."

"Old T.B. won't get any decision over yours truly."

"You can't argue a call."

In 1921, the Giants sponsored an old timer's "tribute game" for Big Six. The headliners included former teammates Larry Doyle, Moose

McCormick, Fred Merkle, Frank Bowerman, Iron Man McGinnity, Art Devlin, Hooks Wiltze, and Roger Bresnahan.

"We hold one dream of vanished years," wrote Grantland Rice, "when Manny's arm was young."

Harry Stevens, the veteran Giants' peanut and scorecard vendor, co-chaired the event with Fred Lieb.

"Nothing we can do is too great for Matty," said Stevens. "I really love that guy."

Lieb, a sportswriter who would live long enough to become a celebrated baseball historian, had to fend off colleague Heywood Broun, who suggested a great idea to boost attendance would be to hold a rattlesnake race between innings.

"Not very dignified," said Lieb. "McGraw would have gone nuts."

Even with no snakes, more than $45,000 was raised for Matty's medical expenses.

"With such support," Christy telegraphed, "I cannot fail to win my game."

And he did . . . or so it seemed.

In late summer, having just turned 41, Matty began a regimen of hiking in the Adironacks, accompanied by Jane, Son, and Polo Grounds the dog. Matty was definitely recovering. "These are some of the happiest days of my life," he told Jane.

In the spring of 1922, Matty threw out the first ball of the Saranac Lake baseball season. With the Adirondacks as his front yard, he focused on studying flowers, often comparing his findings with classmate Lewis Theiss, who was now the editor of publications for the National War Garden Commission. In a note from Lewisburg, Matty found out that he had been elected the first president of the Bucknell "B" Club.

The charmingly quaint town of Saranac, once a poor farming community, now thrived with an economic base of health care and tourism. Christy spent hours in the lobby of the St. Regis Hotel, playing checkers against visitors from across the nation. Yes, he would often play blindfolded. He even defeated Newell Banks, the reigning world checkers champion.

In the fall of 1922, Christy was able to visit his parents in Factoryville. He praised Babe Ruth for commanding an incomprehensible $52,000 contract from the Yankees, joking that he would surely have loved to pitch against the Babe.

Skeptics might suggest that Ruth was hardly worth that kind of cash, having tanked in the '22 World Series with a dismal .118 batting average and no home runs. While the Sultan of Swat would have plenty of great postseasons to come, this would prove to be John McGraw's third and final World Series title.

Matty listened to the games on his new radio, his old friends Grantland Rice and W.O. McGeehan calling the action. It was the first year the World Series would be broadcast, the new marvel of mass communications vaulting from a single AM outlet in 1921 to 556 stations within two years.

In December 1922, Christy was the key speaker at the Christmas Tuberculosis Seals Benefit in New York City's Wannamaker Auditorium.

"I know I'm going to get stage fright," he said from behind the curtain. "I'm beginning to feel embarrassed already."

However, on this night, he was a natural.

"Not a bad place, Saranac," he told the packed crowd. "I lead the life of a country gentleman. Sometimes I ride in the morning and walk in the afternoon. Sometimes I walk in the morning and ride in the afternoon."

At the same time, he did not downplay his battle against the dreaded disease.

"It's the hardest job I ever tackled in my life," he told the audience. "If I could just get out on that old diamond again."

The world seemed to be moving quicker than the old days, Lt. James H. Doolittle of the Army Air Corps having flown from Florida to California in less than 22 hours. Half the nation now lived in cities, fast cars and automobile trails providing a new and expansive freedom. Goodness, the Lincoln Highway stretched from New York City to San Francisco. Sinclair Lewis wrote that George Babbitt's "motor car was poetry and tragedy, love and heroism. The office was his pirate ship, but the car his perilous excursion ashore."

With the approaching spring of 1923, Christy had another long talk with Jane about something she did not want to hear. Offered a part ownership with the Boston Braves, he was to be named team president. Jane, the doctors, anyone who understood the horrendous power of tuberculosis warned against the idea. But Christy was driven, which, as Jane said, was precisely the problem. Matty may have been an outstanding businessman, but he was still weak. He walked with a cane, could not see without glasses, and became easily fatigued. Jane knew he would give every ounce to his work. She knew the nature of the game . . . she knew the stress . . . she knew he would give too much.

He listened to her arguments and signed the contract.

It was exciting to be on the ground floor of rebuilding a baseball franchise, the dead-last Braves having suffered 100 losses in 1922. In fact, Babe Ruth's "disappointing" 35-homer output that season for the Yankees was still three more than the entire Braves team.

Christy would represent the Braves at National League meetings and be involved in trades, acquisitions, and salaries. He could continue to live in Saranac and only travel as his health permitted.

On Opening Day of the 1923 season, the Braves visited the New York Giants. Christy's good friend, Grantland Rice, covered the game for the *New York Herald*:

> "A king walked out of the shadows of the past into the brilliant spring sunshine of the Polo Grounds yesterday as 30,000 loyal subjects paid him the tribute of a roaring acclaim that no crowned monarch could ever know."

To boost the pitching staff in '23, Christy orchestrated a trade with the Giants for his former pupil, Jesse Barnes. It hardly mattered. With a wretched 54-100 record, the Braves would finish seventh in the standings and last in attendance.

Christy at his new home in Saranac.

In 1924, the construction of their brick home at 21 Old Military Road in Saranac Lake was completed. Beautiful and spacious, it had five bedrooms, three baths, and a living room that spelled instant comfort. Christy enjoyed reading by the fireplace or sitting on the porch in his "cure chair." The view and fresh air again brought tranquility, as did the baseball memorabilia and photos on the wall – college days, the 1905 Giants, John and Blanche.

Regarding baseball in Boston, Matty was beginning to realize that he should have listened to Jane. Once again he was tired, handing the daily operations of the presidency to Emil Fuchs as the Braves tumbled back to the cellar, the club's third straight season with exactly 100 losses.

In the fall, the three Mathewsons journeyed to Bucknell, Christy Jr. an incoming freshman prepared to study electrical engineering. The salutatorian of his graduating class at Saranac Lake High School, Christy Jr. had wowed the commencement crowd with a short talk on "Development of Water Power." His goal was to someday blaze a career in wireless telegraphy.

It was doubtful he would follow his father.

"He is a great fan and likes to play the game with the boys," said Matty, "but he is not what I would call a 'bug.' I want him to choose his field."

"He may become President or something like that," added Jane, "but not another Matty. There can't be two like him in the family."

It had been a quarter of a century since Christy and Jane had studied at Bucknell, the new Class of 1927 boasting 337 students. In all, according to the 1924 school catalogue, there were now 963 undergraduates from 18 states and four foreign countries. About the only thing that had not changed was that dad's old math professor, William Cyrus Barton, was still on the faculty. John Howard Harris also remained on campus, but was now a professor of philosophy, having retired as president in 1919.

Bucknell's tuition was $100 in '24, plus another $130 for room and board. It was fortunate that Christy Jr. was such an extraordinary student.

Matty felt a resurgence of energy; that he could now push a bit harder. He attended the 1924 World Series, disheartened as the Giants fell in seven games to Walter "Big Train" Johnson and the Washington Senators. The following spring, Christy caught a common cold on the train to the Braves' spring training camp in St. Petersburg, Florida. It would not get better. Returning to Saranac Lake, he began to suffer blistering pain with each cough.

In April, John Howard Harris died just shy of his 78th birthday. The funeral was in Scranton, but Christy was too sick to attend.

For Matty, every breath became a reminder that death was now, without doubt, closing fast. Finally, he was unable to lift himself from bed, barely able to move at all.

On October 7, 1925, Christy called Jane to his side. He told her what train she should take to Lewisburg, that she needed a private drawing room.

"It's nearly over," he said. "Go out and have a good cry. Don't make it a long one. This is something we can't help."

Jane held his hand.

"Are you sure you are all right?" he whispered to her . . . his last words.

He died of tuberculosis pneumonia the evening of the first game of the World Series between the Pirates and Senators. The flags at Forbes Field were lowered to half-mast. Walter Johnson heard the news as he was walking to the mound. "The Big Train openly wept."

The nation was stunned, every newspaper in the land with deepest remembrance. "He was loved as no other American athlete has ever been loved" (*Oklahoma City Oklahoman*) . . . "An even finer hero in the field of life" (*Boston Traveler*) . . . "There is sorrow felt beyond the realm of baseball" (*Harrisburg Patriot*) . . . "More than a great athlete, he was a great soul" (*Minneapolis Herald*) . . .

The *Saranac Lake Evening Public*:

> "Mathewson's death came as a particularly heavy shock to the residents of this village. The famous pitcher was a familiar figure on the street. He made friends among all classes, journeying from cottage to cottage to indulge his hobby, checkers."

"He was a big man," wrote sportswriter Hugh Fullerton. "Big in body and in mind and about the squarest fellow you ever met."

"How we loved to play for him," said Jack "Chief" Meyers. "We'd break out necks for the guy. If you made an error behind him or anything of that sort, he'd never get mad or sulk. He'd come over and pat you on the back. He had the sweetest, most gentle nature. Gentle in every way."

Early in World War I – on the bloody plains of France – a soldier wrote a poem about sacrifice, remembrance, and rebirth. Where thousands of young men had died, red poppies abundantly grew "In Flanders Fields."

Its seeds may be dormant for years, but when the earth is churned, the red poppy will grow once again.

From Pittsburgh, where they were attending the World Series, the McGraws rushed to Saranac Lake to be with Jane. At Christy's wish, they would bring his body back to his old college home next to the Susquehanna River.

When the train left the Saranac station, hundreds stood silently on the platform. Even more gathered at each depot along the route to Lewisburg, where the Bucknell student body gathered at the edge of town to escort the body to the Stoughton home, a silent parade of grief. The Cameron House (Lewisburg Hotel) was packed, many visitors finding lodging at the University or private homes.

The funeral service was held at the Stoughton home, filled with flowers from across the nation. Pastor Frank Everitt of the Presbyterian Church remarked that Christy looked like "a sun crowned man at peace." The old coach, John McGraw, was visibly shaken, tears streaming from his weathered eyes.

"From an awkward kid, I watched him grow into the most finished artist in the world," said McGraw. "He had strength, intellect, and an uncanny memory. He gave our profession a dignity that it badly needed. He fully realized his early faults and worked constantly to overcome them. He did not want to be regarded as a hero. His was a natural dignity."

It was a Saturday in Lewisburg. All of the stores in town were closed and the Bucknell football game against George Washington was delayed until late afternoon so students could pay their respects. Standing with the kings of baseball and sport, townspeople lined the streets, flags silently draped at half-mast.

At the Lewisburg Cemetery, Son stood by his mother's side, Christy's casket covered with white orchids and red roses. It had been a wonderful life, a long and unbearable struggle.

Jane mentioned the poison gas that her husband had inhaled during World War I.

"I believe that he gave his life for his country," she said, "just as many boys who were killed overseas."

Ernest Sterling, the best man at Christy's wedding, was a pallbearer, as was McGraw and four dignitaries from the Braves, including Emil Fuchs. There were players, umpires, managers, reporters, classmates, students, and professors. There were relatives from Factoryville, friends from throughout the nation. Ty Cobb, who never attended funerals, hid within the crowd of black.

"Matty was a hero of mine," said Ty. "He was truly magnificent in every way."

Down in Washington D.C., they played taps before the third game of the World Series, players from the Senators and Pirates wearing black armbands.

From the *New York Herald*:

> "Let none of us insult the memory of Christy Mathewson by making of him one of those sanctimonious and insufferably perfect heroes. He was a man's man. In all of sport, there never was such an influence for good, such an inspiration for young men. When they are asking who did most for baseball, they will have to say that the man was Christy Mathewson. Sport never will find his like again."

Afterwards, they covered Christy's gravesite with red poppies.

CHAPTER SIXTEEN

April 9, 1929 . . . Bucknell University

Distant clouds were threatening as a small aircraft circled Old Main and Tustin Gym before descending upon the Bucknell baseball field.

Practice disrupted, Coach John Plant's ball club watched in amazement as the Waco 10 made a perfect landing at the edge of the diamond. Exiting the plane, a tall and athletic-looking pilot wearing a long leather coat and flying helmet, waved to the players.

"Just wanted to wish you a great season, boys," the dashing aviator bellowed.

The Bison players immediately knew the air ace . . .

Christy Mathewson Jr. was born to be a hero.

Forever compared to the legendary Big Six, the son carried many of his father's traits. They were dynamic, confident and held a competitive spirit that modestly embraced glory and courageously defied defeat. The story of their lives was always front-page news.

At Bucknell, Christy Jr. studied electrical engineering, was involved with student government and his father's old fraternity, Phi Gamma Delta. An exceptional musician and varsity tennis player, "Cricket" was described in the *L'Agenda* yearbook "one of the most popular students on campus."

"Everybody liked Christy," said classmate Anna Outwater Day, the last living member of the Class of 1927. "All of the memories I have of him are that he was a wonderful person. He was fun, friendly, and mixed in with everybody. He never seemed to think of himself as important just because of his father. Like the girls say these days, he was hot."

"He was drop-dead handsome," said Betty Cook of Lewisburg, a close friend with Jane in later years. "Women were thrilled when he'd ask them to dance."

Just over six feet tall with blue eyes and brown hair, Christy was quite athletic, although he shied away from baseball in favor of tennis, golf, and swimming.

But he did play one ballgame for the Bison varsity. In May 1926, with many of his relatives in the crowd, he started in centerfield. *The Milton Standard* wondered if "it was a dying wish of his father that encouraged Mathewson to take up the great national game." And now, the newspaper predicted, "baseball fans the world over would be rooting hard for the younger Mathewson."

The son harbored no such dreams, having been talked into the venture by manager Walter Blair, the former Highlanders/Yankees catcher and longtime friend of the family.

"But wouldn't be awful to have fans always pointing me out as my great dad's son," said Christy Jr. "It wouldn't be me, you see. Anyway, you don't know how awful a baseball player I am."

He would retire after one game.

The biggest story of 1927 occurred in May when Charles A. Lindbergh Jr., just 25 years old, flew the Spirit of St. Louis non-stop across the Atlantic Ocean, New York to Paris, in 33 hours and 39 minutes. About the same time, Christy Jr. took his first flight, with good friend Eugene Keet piloting from Curtiss Field in Long Island.

Also in May, Christy Jr. graduated Cum Laude from Bucknell. Jane arrived from Saranac Lake, accompanied by John and Blanche McGraw. Although many of the relatives attended, Julia Stoughton was the only grandparent, Frank Stoughton having passed away several years earlier. When Christy died in 1925, his mother had not been able to shake her grief. Four months later, Minerva Mathewson died in Factoryville at the age of 70. Gilbert Mathewson, nearing 80 and in the final year of his life, was too frail to travel.

Christy Jr. had a huge crowd of family and friends, including Lewis Theiss. One of his father's closest friends for all those years and the prolific writer of aviation books, Professor Theiss was now head of the Bucknell journalism department. Theiss presented young Christy with a copy of his latest book, *Piloting the US Air Mail; Flying for Uncle Sam.*

After graduation, Christy Jr. accepted a position as a researcher for General Electric in Schenectady, New York, and immediately took his first flying lesson.

While visiting the Philadelphia home of his best friend, Arthur Phillips, he met Art's sister, Margaret. She was a beautiful, 19-year-old student at Beaver College in Jenkintown. Peggy and Christy fell in love.

On June 5, 1928, the Christy Mathewson Memorial Gateway was dedicated at Bucknell. A gift from professional baseball to honor Big Six, the inscription across the top of the gateway reads, "Athlete—Soldier—Gentleman."

Dignitaries at the ceremony included a large group of players, owners, the presidents of both leagues, and the commissioner of baseball, Judge Kennesaw Mountain Landis. Jane and Christy Jr. also sat on stage as the commissioner made the presentation to the university.

"Matty had more than playing ability to carry him to the heights," said Landis. "It was his character, his integrity, and his heart which endeared him to every man and woman, boy and girl between the two oceans. He was the man who made baseball the truly national game it is today."

There also had been talk of a rotunda to be built on campus, including the possibility of creating a future Baseball Hall of Fame.

After the ceremony had ended, Christy Jr. announced his plan to leave General Electric and forge a new career . . . flying airplanes. His first choice would be to join the Army Air Corp, but he also mentioned that mail pilots could earn nearly $1,000 a month.

It should not have been any surprise that his mother, her sisters, and seemingly everyone else on both sides of the family opposed the notion.

The boy was undoubtedly caught up in the Charles Lindberg craze, the barnstorming exploits of Eddie Rickenbacker, or perhaps he had just read too many books by Lewis Theiss.

But Christy's love of flying went much deeper, having grown up with a thirst for adventure, mechanics, and the skies.

"I like the idea of being up in the air," he said. "I always wanted to fly."

He also – unlike his father – was a very smooth talker, ever alert to unleash that sweet and wonderful smile into the conversation. Eventually he would win their understanding.

"At first, my mother didn't like my idea so much," he said, "but she was awfully nice about it."

"His mother worshipped him," recalled Betty Cook many years later. "After his father died, all her love and interest went to her son. I think he was probably pretty spoiled."

He did not tell his mother about his latest adventure with Eugene Keets, the beginner pilots flying from Schenectady to Elmira.

"We had to fly through three snowstorms," Christy recalled, "following a railroad track, sometimes through ravines. And once the tracks went into a tunnel, and we had to pull a pretty stiff zoom to get over the hill."

On their return trip to Schenectady, they ran into a fourth snowstorm.

"To add to that, our motor began missing. So we landed in the roughest air I've ever been in, and an automobile mechanic in a little town fixed up our engine."

In July 1930, Christy completed advanced training at Kelly Field in San Antonio, Texas, graduating with honors to become a U.S. Army attack pilot.

"Here is for many tail spins and safe landings," Lieutenant Mathewson wrote to Al Stoughton, Bucknell alumni secretary and his cousin.

"These were still the early years of aviation," said Cook, "so he was viewed by everyone as a real adventurer."

Stationed at Mitchell Field in Long Island, Christy Jr. again had to shake the baseball questions.

"They have a baseball team here at the post and I suppose next spring they'll ask me to help out, but I'm afraid I won't be of much use

154

to them," he said before pointing to an airplane. "There, I am able to do something on my own."

Christy Jr. and students in China.

He would definitely put a personal stamp on his next assignment. In light of the Japanese invasion of Manchuria and growing concern of war, the lieutenant was given a three-year tour to help build the Chinese air force. Assigned to Shanghai and later Hangchow, Christy and 15 other American pilots taught young Chinese Nationalists how to fly.

For Christy, life was good, particularly when his fiancé of four years agreed to travel to China for their marriage.

Margaret Phillips, accompanied by her future mother-in-law, Jane Mathewson, left Philadelphia on Thanksgiving Day 1932 for a 9,000-mile journey by train and ship, the *Philadelphia Inquirer* reporting that she was "going to China, land of mystery, glamour, and adventure to the man she loved." They arrived in Hangchow the day before an elegant Christmas

Eve wedding. The story headlined society pages throughout the United States.

On January 8, 1933, after a two-week honeymoon in Shanghai, the couple prepared to return to Hangchow, Christy piloting a large Sikorsky amphibian plane.

Friends assembled on the shore of the Whangpoo River, saying that Peggy, 23 years old, was "thrilled with pride and excitement" as she sat next to Christy for her first plane ride.

But 30 seconds into the flight, the huge plane suddenly dove nose downward into the water and crashed on a mudflat. Chinese river men, having witnessed the horrible crash from their small boats, rushed to the murky island. They tried to pull the Mathewsons from the wreckage. He was critical . . . awake, but unable to move . . . his body crushed.

"Never mind me," he pleaded. "Look after my wife."

It was too late. Peggy would be pronounced dead within a few hours and newspapers across the world reported that he was near death . . . broken arms, shattered legs, internal injuries, head badly cut and bruised. He fought.

Deep in a coma, Christy continually called out "Margaret, Margaret." Doctors gave him less than a five percent chance to survive. When he did awaken, he was so fragile that doctors would not tell him that his wife had died.

Confined for six months in a Shanghai hospital, his left leg would be amputated two inches above the knee and doctors predicted he would never regain full use of his arms. Certainly, he would never again fly.

In late May 1933, Jimmy Doolittle visited Christy in the hospital to wish him well and talk about aviation. A major in the Army reserves, Doolittle had been intensely involved in air racing, holding several world records.

"I have yet to hear anyone engaged in this work dying of old age," he said before retiring from air racing to a more secure vocation of testing aircraft.

Christy was thrilled by the unexpected visit.

"The doctors promise me I will be out in another month," he said, "and then I want to get back to work."

Doolittle asked the nurses to move Christy to the hospital verandah.

156

"I'll get my bearings outside," he said, "and I'll put on a show."

Piloting a new U.S. Army Curtiss Hawk pursuit plane, Doolittle performed a private stunting exhibition as Christy watched from a wheelchair.

"It will take time," he said, "maybe a long time, but I'll be back in the air again."

Doolittle never left the skies, awarded the Medal of Honor by President Franklin D. Roosevelt during World War II and eventually retiring from the Army as a world-famous general.

But, in 1933, who could predict the horrors that would soon unfold.

With his mother still at his side, Christy Jr. returned to Saranac Lake, learning to walk with an artificial leg. He hunted, fished, and climbed hills until he had regained his strength. His goal was to re-enlist with the Army Air Corps.

"Looking at young Matty," wrote Grantland Rice, a family friend for nearly three decades, "I turned back to the older Matty I had seen face so many tight games in the past without a quiver. And his kid was in a worse spot."

On January 29, 1936, Christy Mathewson was one of five legendary ballplayers elected to the charter class of the new Baseball Hall of Fame. The others were Ty Cobb, Babe Ruth, Honus Wagner, and Walter Johnson. Three years later, the four living members of that first class would all attend the official induction ceremony with the opening of the Cooperstown museum. By then, 21 other greats had been added to the Cooperstown ledger, including John McGraw, who had died just shy of his 62nd birthday on February 25, 1934. Connie Mack, Cy Young, Tris Speaker, and Eddie Collins were also Hall of Famers when the museum opened.

Jane had purposely stayed away from baseball.

"Since his death, I just can't bring myself to attend a game at the Polo Grounds," Jane said privately. "If I looked out on the field, at the pitching box where Christy stood so often, the memories would be too poignant."

But, along with her son, Jane did attend the 1939 dedication, unveiling a bust of her late husband. The Mathewson plaque at the Cooperstown museum reads, "Matty was master of them all."

After the induction ceremonies, the inaugural Hall of Fame baseball game was held, the only one that would feature college teams. Johnny Evers, the old Cubs second sacker, threw out the first pitch, Bucknell falling to St. Lawrence 9-5.

When Germany invaded Poland on the first day of September 1939, Christy Jr. was already writing letters requesting that he be reinstated into the Army. Yes, he was disabled . . . but he could fly . . . he just wanted a chance. His requests were rejected, which only fueled his determination.

While his father's fame certainly opened many doors, the young Mathewson always entered on his own terms. Organizing a flying taxi service in the Adirondacks, he continued his quest for re-enlistment, at last able to impress the top military brass with a flawless solo flight.

"That's determination," said Jane. "Just like his father."

The Army, however, was not encouraging. It was a "ceaseless fight, uphill all the way."

Again, he was rejected. Again, he persisted.

Finally, as America entered World War II, the Air Corps relented. It was a desk job, but Captain Mathewson was ecstatic.

"I expect to be back flying again," he said. "They probably won't let me fly combat ships, but there's no reason I can't fly other types."

The Army also had high expectations, selecting Mathewson in early 1942 to command the Thunderbird Chinese Training Program at Arizona's Luke Field, 15 miles from Phoenix. The headline of the *New York Sun* on May 25, 1942 read, "Like Father, Like Son – Courage." Promoted to Major, Christy helped prepare more than a thousand Chinese combat pilots and crews during the course of the war.

"These young men are eager, attentive, and serious students," he wrote Bucknell President Arnaud Marts, "a virtue, sir, that I am sure you will appreciate."

On Saturday night, January 30, 1943, Christy was a headliner on a national radio broadcast commemorating President Franklin D. Roosevelt's 61st birthday and the "March of Dimes" campaign against Infantile Paralysis.

The program started in Washington D.C. and ended in Hollywood. From the Great Lakes Naval Training Center in Illinois, Sammy Kaye and his Orchestra teamed with 200 sailors for a special rendition of "Happy Birthday Mr. President." From Honolulu, Chief Petty Officer Artie Shaw and his Navy Band played "Begin the Beguine."

The heart of the broadcast took place in the Arizona desert as Major Mathewson's cadets sang "Happy Birthday" in Chinese. Christy Jr. spoke briefly about the training program he was commanding, predicting that his fighters would soon find "the exact center of Tokyo." Mathewson then introduced his good friend at the air base, Sergeant Gene Autry singing one of FDR's favorite songs, "The Yellow Rose of Texas." Of course, Christy's favorite by the Singing Cowboy was "Back in the Saddle Again."

The Chinese Training Program was but a sector of Luke Field, the largest training base for fighter pilots of the U.S. Army Air Forces. Sergeant Autry did learn a bit of the Chinese language while there, eventually flying a C-47 air transport plane taking military supplies from India to China by way of the Himalayas, a dangerous run known as "The Hump." Christy would have done anything to earn that assignment.

At the conclusion of the war, the Chinese government decorated Mathewson with the Special Badge Cloud Banner in the name of General Chiang Kai-Shek. Now a Lt. Colonel, Christy was transferred to London, where he met and married actress Lola Finch.

After being discharged from military service in 1946, he and his new wife bought a ranch outside San Antonio, Texas, near the base where he had trained to be a combat pilot 15 years earlier.

The summer of 1950 marked the 30th anniversary of the Mathewson family moving to Saranac Lake. Now 70 years old, Jane had lived there for nearly a quarter of a century without her husband.

"Naturally, I cherish the all-too-few years I spent with Christy as the great experience of my life," she said.

Jane's life in Saranac was quiet, content. She had made a small fortune in the stock market after her husband's death, but was quite frugal. She never owned an air conditioner or television . . . still made her own soap.

She loved to read and travel in the winter, particularly to Florida with Blanche and Texas to see her son. She also enjoyed her trips to Lewisburg. But 1950 was a tough year as Jane lost two sisters – Margaret and Annie. Now, her only sibling was Bessie. Of course, Jane had her son. After the war, she had hoped he might settle in New York or Pennsylvania, but accepted San Antonio . . . he did have a wife.

Jane sometimes visited Laughing Larry Doyle in Saranac. A smoker and former coalminer, he was diagnosed with tuberculosis in 1942, five years after the death of his wife, Gertrude. Upon hearing that he was near destitute due to some bad investments, Jane and Blanche decided to establish a "free bed" in honor of Christy at the Trudeau Sanitarium. Larry Doyle had been the first recipient . . . and was on his way to recovery.

Laughing Larry always referred to Jane as "my manager."

But, other than lasting friendships with former players and their wives, Jane stayed far away from the game itself. When John McGraw died, Blanche was given lifetime box seats at the Polo Grounds. Jane would visit Blanche, but never see baseball. It was the same when Ford Frick, then the National League president, sent her a lifetime pass to every stadium . . . she never used it.

Jane had been her husband's fulltime nurse for nearly a quarter of their 22 years of marriage. She had spent nearly two years nursing Christy Jr. back to health after his tragic plane crash. In the winter of

1941, when Son was badly injured in a head-on automobile accident – the result of another car from the opposite direction skidding across the highway on an icy road – Jane rushed to his side . . . and again would help him back to health.

Despite physical and mental exhaustion, Jane was always strong, always selfless, always there.

On August 15, 1950, Christy Jr. was installing an electric dishwasher when a gas explosion swept his ranch house. Alone at the time, he dragged himself out of the basement and somehow drove himself to the nearest San Antonio hospital. He was conscious when he arrived, but 90 percent of his body was badly burned. He died the next afternoon, just 43 years old.

Jane's world once again crashed . . .

Christy's remains would be brought back to the Lewisburg Cemetery to rest next to his father. After the funeral, Jane asked Bessie to live with her at Saranac Lake. But Bessie did not want to leave her friends in Lewisburg.

"Alright," said Jane, "I don't care where I live anymore."

That fall, she left the house she and her husband had built on Old Military Road and moved back to her childhood home.

CHAPTER SEVENTEEN

June 1955 . . . Lewisburg

At first glance, they might not appear as typical best friends. Jane Mathewson, now 75, was half a century older than Betty Cook, a beautiful young woman she had long called the "grandchild we never had."

Today, amidst a conversation that had jumped from local gossip to Dwight D. Eisenhower's White House, the subject was suddenly Moose McCormick. The old Giant and former baseball coach had worked at Bucknell for years. With huge arms and a scruffy voice, his stature could be somewhat intimidating.

"But you know," Betty said to Jane, "he's all bark and no bite. Beneath the grumpiness is a heart of gold."

"If you say so, dear," said Jane, more interested in leafing through her mail than talking about retired baseball players.

Betty and her parents had known Jane for many years. Living three doors down from the Stoughton home on Market Street, they had even driven Jane back to Saranac Lake on several occasions, a two day trip covering 360 miles that had inevitably turned into a vacation . . . what with the huge house on Old Military Road filled with baseball memorabilia, a front yard to the Adirondack Mountains. On one visit in the late '40s, Jane had even introduced a teen-aged Betty to the great singer, Kate Smith.

But now, Jane had been back in Lewisburg for close to five years. With a hint of disapproval, she opened a large white envelope, took a quick glance inside, and tossed it on the table.

"I don't know why they keep sending me these things," she said. "I never go."

"What is it?" asked Betty.

"Oh, it's just another invitation from the Baseball Hall of Fame," said Jane. "I haven't been since that first year in 1939."

Curious, Betty picked up the invitation, her eyes immediately drawn to a cluster of magical words.

"Induction of Joseph Paul DiMaggio?" she blurted. "The Yankee Clipper . . ."

Jane looked up at her young friend, who was now reading aloud the invitation in what could only be described as an emotional frenzy.

"Hall of Fame Exhibition Game with the Boston Red Sox . . . Ted Williams will be there," Betty jabbered. "And the Milwaukee Braves . . . Hank Aaron, Warren Spahn, Eddie Mathews."

Slowing down, Betty began from the beginning.

"The National Baseball Hall of Fame and Museum and the Village of Cooperstown, New York, cordially invite you and a guest to attend the dedication of plaques on Monday, July 25, 1955."

Betty proudly announced the six inductees.

"Dazzy Vance, Ted Lyons, Gabby Hartnett, Ray Schalk, Home Run Baker, and Joltin' Joe DiMaggio."

Smiling, Jane interrupted.

"If you want to go," she said, "we will go."

Jane Stoughton Mathewson.

And so began an adventure that would take place every summer for the next 12 years – 200 miles of back roads from Lewisburg to Cooperstown – Betty driving and Jane riding shotgun.

"Did you ever think about getting married again," Betty once asked her passenger. "I would guess you had many opportunities."

"Oh, my dear, Christy was my husband," said Jane. "No one could have possibly taken his place."

At the 1955 Hall of Fame Induction Ceremony, Commissioner Ford Frick called 40-year-old Joe DiMaggio the "baby of the group." Gabby Hartnett and Ted Lyons were in their mid-50s, Home Run Baker the oldest at 69.

The New York Times reported that DiMaggio "stole the spotlight," but Betty Cook would also meet Ty Cobb, Bill Terry, Frankie Frisch, Mel Ott, and Cy Young.

Approaching the final days of his life, Young was 88, Cobb a spry 20 years younger. Betty found both to be charming.

"According to Jane," said Betty, "Ty had mellowed by that time."

The Times also noted that four famous widows were in attendance at the induction ceremony – Mrs. Christy Mathewson, Mrs. John McGraw, Mrs. Roger Bresnahan, and Mrs. Eddie Collins.

"The men get all the attention," Jane joked. "The women are excess baggage."

As for the 14th annual Hall of Fame exhibition game, Ted Williams slashed a two-run homer as the Red Sox downed the Braves 4-2.

Baseball movies were major box office hits in the 1940s and '50s. In 1942, Gary Cooper played Lou Gehrig in the timeless classic *Pride of the Yankees*. William Bendix starred in the *Babe Ruth Story* in 1948 and James Stewart had a huge hit the following year with *The (Monty) Stratton Story* about the White Sox pitcher who lost a leg but eventually returned to the mound. In 1952, *The Pride of St. Louis* featured Dan Daily as Dizzy Dean. That was the same year Ronald Reagan played Grover Cleveland Alexander, starring with Doris Day in *The Winning Team*.

As can be imagined, *The Christy Mathewson Story* would have been a certain epic blockbuster. Or so thought the Hollywood producers who visited Jane, seeking her permission for the script to be written, a star to be signed, and filming to begin. Jane listened carefully to the proposals. Bottom line, she would not permit it.

In order to enhance their films, she reasoned, the studios took far too many liberties with the truth.

Blanche McGraw must have agreed with Jane's unwillingness to have Christy recreated for the big screen . . . imagine the revisions that would need to be required for a movie about Little Napoleon.

Actually, Lewisburg was one of Blanche's favorite destinations . . . a sometimes needed respite from Manhattan. Blanche had lost little of her youthful spirit. She was fun, educated, and well traveled. She loved to talk and was slow to judge. In fact, it was much easier to see Blanche and Jane as twin sisters from two worlds than to understand the bond between their late husbands.

Over the years, Blanche had become quite close to all of Jane's sisters, particularly Bessie. Like Blanche, Bessie was both a firebrand and lady of fashion.

"Well, look at you, sitting at breakfast like Diamond Lil," Jane would kid her older sister.

"Papa always said that it's a poor house without at least one lady," Bessie would reply.

While Jane might often refuse Blanche's invitations to visit her home at 5th Avenue and 10th Street, Bessie loved the energy of Broadway and the Polo Grounds.

After John McGraw's death in 1934, the Giants honored Blanche with a lifetime box right behind the home dugout. Box 19 had eight seats and was always filled with Blanche and friends. Betty Cook and her mother sometimes visited Blanche, cheering for the likes of Johnny Antonelli, Monte Irvin, Red Schoendienst, Al Dark, Sal "The Barber" Maglie . . . Willie Mays.

Blanche, a longtime stockholder with the Giants, had witnessed some remarkable moments over the years. In 1951, she saw Bobby Thomson's "Shot Heard Round the World" to sink the Brooklyn Dodgers. Remarkably, the blast ended a mad dash in which the Giants somehow erased a 13.5 game deficit in the final weeks of the season, a feat forever known as the "Miracle of Coogan's Bluff." That set up a World Series showdown between the Giants and Yankees, the first postseason for Willie Mays and Mickey Mantle, both rookie sensations. When the teams moved to the Polo Grounds for Game 3, Blanche McGraw threw out the first pitch, the Giants winning 6-2. The Yankees, however, would capture the crown in six games.

The Giants would return to the Fall Classic in '54, sweeping the favored Cleveland Indians, a series forever stamped by "The Catch" of Willie Mays.

The Giants had tumbled to third in 1955, followed by two straight seasons in sixth, but nothing was more heartbreaking for Blanche than the afternoon of September 29, 1957, the last game ever to be played in the Polo Grounds, the franchise moving to San Francisco. Before the game, manager Bill Rigney presented Blanche with a bouquet of red roses. Moose McCormick, Hooks Wiltse, and Rube Marquard were there from the old days, part of a bittersweet gathering of only 11,606 fans. In the bottom of the ninth, as the Pirates sealed a 9-1 romp, both teams rushed for the centerfield locker rooms, trying to outmaneuver the fans rushing onto the field one last time. It was 1908 all over again . . . and then it was quiet.

Documented within the official history of baseball, Blanche McGraw – roses still in her hands – was the last person to leave the Polo Grounds.

Blanche never lost her love for the Giants. In April 1958, she attended the club's first game in San Francisco, played at Seals Stadium. Willie Mays was still the headliner, but a superb group of rookies – Orlando Cepeda, Jim Davenport, Felipe Alou, and Willie Kirkland – helped propel the Giants once again into contenders.

There was no Hall of Fame induction ceremony in '58, but they did play the annual exhibition game at Doubleday Field, the Washington Senators edging the Phillies, 5-4.

Following the game at the Otesaga Hotel, Betty Cook was talking with a group of Phillies players when Jane arrived. Betty made the introduction.

"They about fell over," Betty said. "Everybody assumed that Mrs. Mathewson was dead. They didn't realize that she had been a widow for 33 years. They couldn't believe they were meeting her."

Jack Sanford – a young pitching ace on the Phillies – politely reached for Jane's hand.

"Mrs. Mathewson," he said, "may I ask you a question? I always understood that your husband never drank, smoked, or swore. Just how straight and narrow was Christy?"

"Now Jack," she smiled, "you don't think I would marry such a prude, do you?"

Of course, Jane had heard the question before, many times.

"There was nothing mamby-pamby or sissy about him," she said. "He was a real he-man. He did most of the things other players did, never tried to pose as a paragon of virtue, but no one could be around him long without recognizing the fine stuff in the man, his character, his ability, his inherent sense of decency."

Educated, charming, fun; Jane became known as baseball's "most celebrated and gracious widow," a newspaper adding that "her young friend Betty was the belle of the ball."

"We both were treated like royalty," said Betty.

As was Blanche, keeping Cooperstown and San Francisco on her busy calendar. She would visit San Francisco again in April 1960 for the opening of Candlestick Park and even see the Giants in the '62 World Series, attending all three games played at Yankee Stadium. The Giants had four world titles – 1905, 1921, 1922, 1954 – and Blanche had seen them all. But not a fifth . . . in Game 7 at Candlestick, the Yankees pulled out a 1-0 victory to secure a 20th World Series championship. It would have driven John McGraw crazy.

Less than a month later, on November 5, 1962, Blanche Sindall McGraw passed away at the age of 80.

Soon after Blanche's passing, Bessie Stoughton Cregar entered a nursing home. Now living alone, Jane had an open invitation for dinner at the home of Betty and her parents.

Edward and Anna Cook – both about the age of Jane's son – owned a huge three-story brick home that had been built in 1844, originally housing Lewisburg's first bank.

"We had air conditioning and a color TV," said Betty. "Jane never missed Mitch Miller or Bonanza. She had a great sense of humor. She was part of the family."

Jane decided to will Christy's memorabilia to the Baseball Hall of Fame in Cooperstown and Keystone College in Factoryville. Meanwhile, she often donated significant gifts to the Presbyterian Church and Bucknell University, establishing the Jane and Christy Mathewson Memorial Scholarship. She also made donations to Phi Gamma Delta . . . in fact she still wore the fraternity pin that Christy had given to her in 1901 on all formal occasions.

Jane carried herself with great dignity, a deep love for husband and son that time could not weather. She had a strong faith and dedication to her church. There was reading, travel, a sewing bee, talking with Bucknell students and her many friends, riding around town in Betty's convertible and their yearly trips to the Hall of Fame induction ceremony. Despite the burdens of old age, she created a life that was comfortable and good.

"People were always drawn to her," said Betty. "She was so charming."

It was summer 1966 in Cooperstown, Jane sitting in a rocking chair on the front porch of the Ostesage Hotel talking with her good friend, Claire Ruth. Casey Stengel, who was to be inducted with Ted Williams, stopped by and recalled his early years with Brooklyn, his inability to hit Big Six.

"Mrs. Mathewson was queen of the night, though she was unaware of it and the designation would horrify her," wrote Hall of Fame curator Ken Smith. "She was a woman of warmth and wisdom with a gentle spirit. We loved her."

Jane Stoughton Mathewson was 87 years old when she threw out the first pitch to dedicate Lewisburg's new Wolfe Field in the spring of 1967. It would be her last public appearance. She passed away on May 29 . . . Memorial Day.

Once again, people arrived from across the nation, including a large contingent of friends from the Hall of Fame.

The three Mathewsons are buried side by side on a beautiful hill in the Lewisburg Cemetery, within a stone's throw of Bucknell.

SELECTED BIBLIOGRAPHY

Allen, Lee. *The National League Story* (1965)

Asinof, Eliot. *1919: America's Loss of Innocence* (1991)

Asinof, Eliot. *Eight Men Out* (1963)

Buford, Kate. *Native American Son: The Life and Sporting Legend of Jim Thorpe* (2010)

Claudy, C.H. *The Battle of Base-Ball* (1912)

DeFord, Frank. *The Old Ball Game* (2006)

Fleming, G.H. *The Unforgettable Season* (1981)

Graham, Frank. *The New York Giants* (1952)

Gutman, Bill. *They Made It A Whole New Ball Game* (1977)

Harris, John Howard. *Thirty Years as President of Bucknell* (1926)

Hartley, Michael. *Christy Mathewson: A Biography* (2004)

Hynd, Noel. *The Giants of the Polo Grounds* (1988)

Keller, Jane E. *Adirondack Wilderness: A Story of Man and Nature* (1980)

Lieb, Fred. *Baseball As I Have Known It* (1977)

Light, Jonathan F. *The Cultural Encyclopedia of Baseball* (1997)

Lord, Walter. *The Good Years, From 1900 to the First World War* (1960)

Masur, Louis P. *Autumn Glory: Baseball's First World Series* (2003)

Mayer, Ronald A. *Christy Mathewson: A Game-by-Game Profile* (1993)

Mathewson, Christy. *Pitching in a Pinch* (1912)

McGraw, Blanche Sindall. *The Real McGraw* (1953)

McGraw, John. *My Thirty Years In Baseball* (1923)

Murphy, Cait. *Crazy '08* (2007)

Newcombe, Jack. The Fireballers (1964)

Ritter, Lawrence. *The Glory of Their Times* (1966)

Robertson, John G. *Baseball's Greatest Controversies* (1995)

Robinson, Ray. *Matty: An American Hero* (1993)

Schoor, Gene. *Christy Mathewson: Baseball's Greatest Pitcher* (1953)

Seib, Philip. *The Player* (2003)

Smith, Robert. *Heroes of Baseball* (1952)

Stark, Benton. *The Year They Called Off The World Series* (1991)

Wallace, Joseph. *The Baseball Anthology: 125 Years* (1994)

ABOUT THE AUTHOR

Born into a naval family, Robert Gaines was raised in California, Rhode Island, and Virginia. Even as a child, he had an obsession for recording his stray thoughts into hundreds of notebooks.

After graduating from San Diego State, Bob became a sportswriter and columnist for a large daily newspaper in San Diego. In the early 1990s, he left California to become manager of development communications at Bucknell University in Lewisburg, PA. He edited *The Beauty of Bucknell* (Harmony House, 2001 and was the key writer for hundreds of university publications, plus writing and producing several Bucknell documentaries.

Gifted with excellent social skills, Bob became a university fundraiser before taking early retirement in 2009 to focus on writing. Bob has a number of writing projects, all different in scope, that are soon to be published.

COMPLETED WORKS OF FICTION

The Man With Total Control was written in the early '70s about a lost and socially inept man locked within the shelter of his home. Jeremy Mueller wishes he could open the door and leave, but knows he never will.

The Brave Historian, a study in perfection about a man approaching 100, one last chance to realize his distant dream of fame. It is a deep and unique novel about a mind that never stops and distant memories too vivid to shake.

The Chronicles of Loose – A funny and poignant tale about two dogs of the '70s – the beautiful golden lab, Sundance, and his sidekick, the odd and straggly Loose, who, convinced he is from another universe, does all the talking though nobody seems to be listening.

One Christmas Lasts Forever is a touching dream that unites – for one beautifully strange night – a father's two young children with the lost relatives of his boyhood.

COMPLETED WORKS OF NON-FICTION

The Colored Halfback is the true story of Andrew Heidelberg, the first African-American to play "white" high school football in the south. The book and screenplay – written with Andrew – are both being proposed to major publishing companies and movie studios.

Go Down West Virginia is the story of Robert Y. Gaines (Bob's father), who miraculously survived Pearl Harbor. He was strong, intelligent, and reserved, with a marvelous wit he seldom revealed. When the author was 25 years old and his father a Naval captain, he found the battle-ship scrapbook from the summer of 1941. The ancient photos showed his father and buddies as fun and energetic sailors on the U.S.S. West Virginia. "Who are these guys?" Bob asked his mother. "Oh, they're all dead," she said. "They all died at Pearl Harbor." Suddenly, he understood his father's silence.

ACKNOWLEDGEMENTS

The Baseball Hall of Fame (Cooperstown, NY) – Tim Wiles, Director of Research, and Freddy Berowski, Reference Librarian.

Bucknell University (Lewisburg, PA) – Jon Terry, Director of Sports Information.

Keystone College (La Plume, PA) – Terry N. Wise, Associate Professor, Sport & Recreation Management

To my family and friends . . .

For further information on Christy Mathewson and his family, visit: www.3mathewsons.com

Made in the USA
Charleston, SC
21 May 2012